Whimpering in
the Rhododendrons

ARTHUR MARSHALL was educated at a Hampshire prep school, Oundle and at Christ's College, Cambridge. He was a master and housemaster at Oundle from 1931-54, departing only to join the Intelligence Corps during the war. After serving as private secretary to Lord Rothschild he became a full-time journalist and broadcaster in 1964. He has written for the *Sunday Telegraph*, *Punch*, the *Listener*, the *Times Literary Supplement*, the *New Statesman*, the *Standard* and the *Spectator*. He is the author of several books, including *Girls Will Be Girls* (1974) and *I'll Let You Know* (1981).

D0778031

Whimpering in the Rhododendrons

The Splendours and Miseries
of the English prep school

ARTHUR MARSHALL

Drawings by Tim Jaques

FONTANA/Collins

First published by William Collins Sons & Co. Ltd 1982
First issued in Fontana Paperbacks 1983

Copyright © Arthur Marshall 1982
Copyright © in drawings Tim Jacques 1982

Made and printed in Great Britain by
William Collins Sons & Co. Ltd, Glasgow

Contents

List of Contributors
Foreword   5

Back to School   7
7.15 a.m.   21
8 a.m.   34
8.15 a.m.   53
9 a.m.   64
10 a.m.   80
11 a.m.   89
Sunday noon   95
1 p.m.   107
2 p.m.   117
2.30 p.m.   136
4 p.m.   149
6 p.m.   160
Bedtime   166
Day's End   172

List of Contributors

Works and More by Max Beerbohm (John Lane, The Bodley Head 1930). *St Andrew's School 1877–1977* by Paul Spillane (Hobbs, Southampton 1977). *The Puppet Show of Memory* by Maurice Baring (Heinemann 1922). *First Childhood* by Lord Berners (Constable 1934). *Through Irish Eyes* by The Hon. Terence Prittie (Backman & Turner 1977). *Our Family Affairs* by E. F. Benson (Cassell 1920). *A Century of Summer Fields* by R. Usborne (Methuen 1964). *Cradle of Empire* by Meston Batchelor (Phillimore 1981, Blackwell Press). *Oranges at Half-Time* by Eustan More (J. M. Dent 1967). *A Dragon Century 1877–1977* by C. H. Jaques (Blackwells 1977). *Sisyphus & Reilly* by Peter Luke (Deutsch 1972). Col. H. P. Whitefoord, extracts from 'Petticoat Government' printed in GKN Trade Magazine, Summer 1959. *Time Was* by Graham Robertson (Hamish Hamilton 1931). *On the psychology of military incompetence* by Norma F. Dixon (Futura 1979). *Meditations of a Broomstick* by Lord Rothschild (Collins 1977). *Lost Lectures* by Maurice Baring. *Salisbury History* by P. L. Smith in The Hatcher Review, Number 10.

Noel Currer-Briggs, Patrick Davis, Humphrey Percy, H. M. S. Man, C. A. Grundy, J. Montgomery, Denys Watkins, Thomas Wright, Leigh Jennings, Mrs A. J. Percy, John Pritchard, Ian English, Dan Symonds, Dr C. L. Davidson, N. C. S. Down, Mrs Gee, Hugh & Charles Riley, Mrs Woolf, Carinthia Arbuthnot Lane, Allan Ledger, Mrs Ann Mcnaught-Davis, Peter Bull, Tudor Trevor, Mrs Needham, Colin Shaw, Gareth Moore, Hugh Pratt, Patrick MacLoughlin and G. R. Dampier-Bennett.

Foreword

The book that follows is an affectionate and in no way a serious and scholarly study of preparatory schools, those establishments that cope with the educational and physical needs of boys between, roughly, the ages of eight and thirteen, boys whose parents can afford the fees and who usually have in mind their sons' onward progress to a public school. Some refer to such schools as 'private schools', which indeed most of them are, but here we have kept to the more usual word, 'prep' schools.

The modern prep school has to be efficient to live and present-day standards are admirably high, with excellent modern buildings and a much wider curriculum than hitherto, both in and out of the classroom. The majority of staffs are dedicated and hard-working and the day of the sadistic autocrat is long since past. But in recounting the *splendeurs et misères* of any institution, it is – such is human nature – with the *misères* that interest mainly lies.

Our book has been chiefly compiled from the varied experiences of former prep school boys. They have kindly recalled and generously supplied for our interest and pleasure – and, in some cases, total astonishment – facts and details from their school years. A list of these bene-factors will be found opposite. The book is an attempt to recapture, in a fairly light-hearted manner, the feel and spirit of such schools before, as seems quite likely, all but the best vanish for ever.

Lord Berners was far from happy at his prep school, a pretty grim one called Elmley and of which we shall be hearing more, but after many years had passed by he decided, just for interest and with no rancour in his heart, to return to it for a visit and to see how things were going. There it all was, just as he so clearly remembered – the square Georgian house, the asphalt playground, the elms and the playing-fields – but he noticed immediately a different and new atmosphere about the place, one of cheerfulness and a carefree gaiety that had been noticeably missing in the old days. And he then discovered that the school was a school no longer and had become instead a private lunatic asylum. Some will find this less peculiar than others.

Author's Note

In order to give the very varied subject matter some form and shape, and to allow readers an occasional breather, the contents has been spread over an average day in the life of an average prep school. The activities taking place under the different times of day are, roughly, the normal routine in most such schools.

Back to School

The other evening, at about seven o'clock, I was in a swift hansom. My hat was tilted at a gay angle, and, for all I was muffled closely, my gloves betokened a ceremonious attire. I was smoking *la cigarette d'appétit* and was quite happy. Outside Victoria my cab was stopped by a file of other cabs, that were following one another in at the main entrance of the station. I noticed, on one of them, a small hat-box, a newish trunk and a corded playbox, and I caught one glimpse of a very small pale boy in a billicock-hat. He was looking at me through the side-window. If Envy was ever inscribed on any face, it was inscribed on the face of that very small, pale boy. 'There,' I murmured, 'but for the grace of God, goes Max Beerbohm!'

The date of Beerbohm's essay on 'Going Back to School' is 1899 (he was on his way, as a distinguished critic, to a theatre *première*, with perhaps dinner at Frascati's to follow) but the situation and the sentiments might belong to any subsequent year, as is shown by the *cris de coeur* so generously and even gladly supplied and cried for us by ex-schoolboys in the pages that follow. The pale-faced boy

was perhaps setting out for some Surrey school, for the
hour was hardly suitable for anything further afield, and
would be shepherded with other victims from Platform 3
by a jovial junior master. Was the boy's mother with him
in the hansom? We are not told but the newness of that
trunk makes one think that perhaps she was. Mothers on
platforms and at goodbye moments are perilous and
potentially embarrassing material.

In some cases the headmaster himself did the shepherd-
ing from London and here is the celebrated Mr E. L.
Browne in action:

> The tiny boy at Victoria Station, confronted by
> this elephantine figure, with a white mane of hair,
> rosy weatherbeaten face, vast moustache, twinkling
> eyes and genial smile, was often too overwhelmed
> by the aura of dignity and strength to gain much
> reassurance from such welcoming remarks as,
> 'Laddie, ye are leaving home for the first time, and
> entering strange surroundings, but if ye keep your
> ears and eyes open and your mouth shut ye won't
> go very far wrong.' But these words of advice were
> sympathetically given, if not so received.
>
> Parents sometimes found him equally alarming.
> The fussy ones got no encouragement from him,
> and he often spoke to them with a certain bluntness,
> from which the cheerful smile and level voice
> removed any cause for offence: 'Now you know as
> well as I do that you have no business to ask for
> that.' At Victoria, when an anxious mother of a new
> boy proposed to come and visit her son in the first
> fortnight of term 'to soften the sudden change from
> home', he replied, 'If you had a puppy, would you
> cut off its tail an inch at a time or do it all at once?'

He had a disconcerting method of dealing with pertinacious parents whose enquiries were ill-timed or obtuse, as is shown by the following conversation which took place on the long asphalt when he was surrounded by boys and parents:

'Well, Mr Browne, how is my boy getting on?'
'He stands up to fast bowling very well.'
'Yes, but in other ways how is he doing?'
'I think he is developing a natural off-break.'

Panicky telegrams were not encouraged. One Monday morning a mother telegraphed, 'No letter this morning. How is Peter?' E.L.B. replied, 'Very well, thank you. How are you?'

For a boy's arrival for his first term at his prep school, parental accompaniment was usually considered essential.

We arrived about tea-time. The school was a red brick building on the top of the hill, north of Ascot Station and situated among pine trees. We were shown into a drawing-room where the headmaster and his wife received us with a dreadful geniality. There was a small aquarium in the room with some goldfish in it. The furniture was covered with black-and-yellow cretonne, and there were some low ebony bookcases and a great many knick-knacks. Another parent was there with a small and pale-looking little boy called Arbuthnot, who was the picture of misery, as I saw at a glance that he was wearing a made-up sailor's tie. Two days later the machinery inside this tie was a valuable asset in another boy's collection. Conversation was kept up hectically until tea was over. They talked of a common friend, Lady Sarah Spencer. 'What a charming woman she is,' said the headmaster. How sensible he seemed to charm! How impervious to all amenities he revealed himself to be later!

The words 'dreadful geniality' are perhaps a little unkind but were written many years later, and with hindsight. Doubtless the headmaster did his best, at what may well have been for him an equally fraught moment, the mother in question being what is known as 'well connected' and influential. So he made with the Earl Grey and the Dundee cake and the cheerful platitudes. One of the latter was often, 'You'll soon find your feet here,' a statement which in my own introduction to prep school life was erroneous, for it took me the full four years to find my feet, by which time my feet were in altogether more pleasant circumstances and at Oundle.

Few prep schools have ever been designed and built as schools. They are usually largish country houses with, concealed in the hinterland, hut-like additions, additions in which corrugated iron has played a major constructional role. Thus, the first view of the establishment was sometimes a misleading one, for the building often had a faintly home-like look.

Elmley was about an hour's journey by train from London. It had been arranged that I should go down early in the day with my mother, so that I might become familiar with my new surroundings before the other boys arrived. The school was quite close to the station. It looked at first sight pleasant enough. A square Georgian House of grey stucco; in front of it a wide asphalt playing-ground enclosed by a low wall and flanked by constructions of more recent date, on one side a rather ugly chapel and on the other a conglomeration of out-houses, fives courts, offices and a swimming bath. The path from the station led through the playing fields. A tall row of elms ran parallel to the house, and on the farther side of it (which was really the front) a group of ilexes and conifers sheltered the house from the main road.

Apprehension must have reduced my personality and magnified external objects; for everything at Elmley appeared to me to be of immense size. The elm trees seemed gigantic, the house of Cyclopean dimensions and the playing fields as vast as the savannahs. For years afterwards I continued to think of everything at Elmley as being over life-size so that when I visited it again in recent years the scenery seemed to have considerably shrunk.

Although headmasters and their wives did their best to make the first encounter friendly and easy, the building in which they did it did not always strike a welcoming note. Many will remember the headmaster's obviously more comfortable quarters in the big house, quarters approached through a green baize door and only when the approacher had been summoned. From this privileged area too there frequently came cooking smells that gave evidence of different diets being consumed beyond.

For a boy's first appearance at his prep school, the correct clothing and equipment were of maximum importance. Which of us who experienced it does not recall, with a shiver of horror, the discovery that one's grey flannel suit seemed to be either lighter or darker than the others? That one's tuck-box was either bigger or smaller?

I went to Sandroyd in 1927. My dear Mama, anxious that I should not put a foot wrong, having got the school clothing list, found that the purple school cap could only be bought at the school itself. As we lived in Yorkshire, she wrote to the headmaster to ask what headgear I should wear. Back came the answer, 'a bowler hat'. So, at the age of eight, clad in thick tweed knickerbockers (everyone else wore plus-fours) and a Norfolk jacket (everyone else wore an ordinary jacket without that awful band and the pleats in the back, which I have always thought must have been designed by a tailor with a spinal curvature which he wished to hide) I joined the train at Waterloo. I was also equipped with a Revelation suitcase in which was packed my 'night requirements'. These consisted of a pair of pyjamas (thick, striped flannel), a camel-hair dressing gown, a thick leather handkerchief box, an equally thick leather Eton collar box, a stud box, a rubber sponge bag with toothbrush, toothpaste, loofah, sponge, and face-flannel, bedroom slippers, a spare pair of pants and vest, a flannel shirt, a pullover and a silver framed portrait of my mother and father. Forty years later I weighed all this and found that it came to just under half a hundred-weight. I shall never forget to my dying day the awful struggle through the pinewoods of Oxshott carrying this frightful impedimenta.

For the under-sized there were additional problems.

My first day at a boarding school was sheer terror. At the age of nine I was four feet high and weighed just over four stone. This helped to create a pro-

nounced inferiority complex. Mentally, I was about average for my age, but suffered from fits of extreme lassitude.

My parents deposited my brother and me at the school. Its appearance was forbidding – the boys of other schools that played games against us called it 'the prison'. All four of us were ushered into the headmaster's part of the gaunt and unprepossessing Victorian building. He and his wife, certainly, seemed ultra-friendly. There may have been a bizarre reason for this; much later in life I learnt that my parents, as 'Honourables' and with a title in the offing, paid reduced fees for us!

I had a hideous sinking feeling when the moment came for my parents to leave. The moment that they left, the head's manner became strictly matter-of-fact.

Although things are better now in the way of amenities for both staff and boys, a hundred years ago it was the headmaster who chiefly benefited from any comforts that were going and who could be relied upon to pamper himself in the matter of accommodation.

After Easter 1878, I was sent to a private school presided over by Mr Ottiwell Waterfield, at Temple Grove, East Sheen, and remained there three years. The house and grounds vanished entirely somewhere about 1908, under the trail of the suburban builder, and now hideous rows of small residences occupy their spaciousness. For the purposes of a school numbering some hundred and thirty boys, the original George and Queen Anne house had been largely supplemented with dormi-

tories and schoolrooms, and a modern wing as
large as the house ran at right angles by the edge of
the cricket field. But the part where Mr Waterfield
and his family lived had not been touched; there
was a fine library, drawing-room and his study (how
awful was that place!) en suite, a paved hall, with a
full-sized billiard-table and a piano where a frail
widow lady called Mrs Russell gave music lessons;
and the French master, whose name really was
M. Voltaire, conducted a dancing-class there as
well as teaching French and being, I think, slightly
immoral. A passage out of the hall gave on to the
private garden of Mr Waterfield, where there were
fine cedar trees and a broad oak staircase led up
from it to the bedrooms of the family.

On the first traumatic day at school, let it not be supposed
that the boy being parentally deposited was the only sufferer.

Twice I have taken a little eight-year-old to
Summer Fields for his first term. I suppose that I
shall never know how miserable they felt. The
crunch begins at the tea-party. There are the
parents trying to keep up bright chatter. And the
little boys are trying to pretend to enjoy the eats
provided. Everybody is keeping a stiff upper lip,
and how! And, in the end, one drives away with
one last look at a forlorn diminutive figure waving
farewell. Is it for the children that our English
boarding schools system is so cruel, or is it for their
parents?

Talking of parents, by and large I do not approve
of Summer Fields parents. On two separate
occasions, in the family relay race on Sports Day, I

have been fouled – I have no reason to doubt
deliberately – by rival parents. Once I was neatly
tripped: once I was nudged in the small of the back.
If it were not for the ridiculous laws of libel in this
country I would name one of them. He has since
become a most distinguished employee of Her
Majesty. I turn a wary and suspicious eye on all
Summer Fields parents.

And some mothers, separating from their young, proved
to be made of even less stern stuff.

The final day was a blur of horror for me. We took
Mallory down to Oxford. We drove to the school.
We had tea with the headmaster. The headmaster
looked at me with compassion. One of the master's
wives told me that the new-comers always came to
her house on Sunday mornings. Matron was brisk.
There were dozens of sandwiches. Dozens of
mothers with hot red eyes; dozens of little boys,
very little boys. Mallory's blond head shone in the
sunlight. I went up to his dormitory. His case had
been unpacked and his little possessions disposed
on a chair. Our photographs, and a particularly
unattractive one of Nanny that he had specially
framed, stood on the chest of drawers. Everyone
was very kind, very understanding. Matron was
comforting. There was more tea, more sandwiches.
The headmaster was drowned in a sea of mothers.
The fathers all looked resolutely at the cricket
pitch. Mallory went out of the french windows and
on to the lawn. It was time to go. I took his warm
dry little hand in mine. I looked down into his
face . . .

Many will recall imperfections in prep schools in their methods of illumination – even after the First World War, oil-lamps were still in use in a remote Hampshire school. Elsewhere dormitories were lit solely by one naked and hissing gas jet, while in classrooms mantled gas gave only a relatively dim light. But gradually another, cleaner form took over.

> There was electric light in the school, and the electric light was oddly enough supposed to be under the charge of one of the boys, who was called the head engineer. Clever and precocious as this boy was, I cannot now believe that his office was a serious one, although we took it seriously indeed at the time. However that may be, nobody except this boy was allowed to go into the engine-shed or to have anything to do with the electric light. We were especially forbidden to touch any of the switches in the house or even to turn on or off the electric light ourselves. One day one of the boys was visited by his parents, and he could not resist turning on the electric light, which in houses at that time was a new thing and few private houses were lighted with it. Unfortunately the head saw him do this through the window, and directly his parents were gone the boy was flogged.

Electric power brought with it, of course, dangers of its own.

> Electricity was not installed until 1929. Indeed, together with central heating, it was considered worthy of special mention in a prospectus of 1930. Paradoxically, it was not naked gas, but an electricity fault that caused a serious fire in the big

schoolroom. Its seriousness, however, is remembered less than the joyous spectacle of the headmaster, in clerical collar, shirt and pyjamatrousers, disappearing, hose in hand, through the floor into the basement thirteen feet below, shortly to re-emerge, like the demon king of pantomime, black-faced and soaking, but entirely unhurt.

One wonders what punishment would have been considered adequate for the following example of flagrant disobedience.

I had just been presented by my parents with an electric motor. It was a wet Sunday afternoon. I asked permission officially to be allowed to connect this motor to the electric lights. This permission was refused on the grounds that I would be using electricity unnecessarily and it would be impossible to compute what I would have to pay to the school for its use. I was also told that I must send the motor back home as soon as possible. This was asking too much of a young boy with a new toy. As soon as the master on duty was out of the room, I plugged the motor into the nearest light socket and promptly fused all the lights.

'The school is illuminated throughout by electric light' was the kind of thing that looked well in the prospectus, that, in many cases, glossy and deceptively attractive document whose motto can only have been *multum in parvo*.

The brochure with which our gullible parents were ensnared was a dream of white linen, sparkling glass, flowers on tables and on the gay counterpanes in airy dormitories, together with clean, unnatural looking boys in Eton suits. The staff consisted of the headmaster and his wife, two assistant masters and a matron/cook. There was also a gardener for the 'grounds'. We accepted the fact that there was a simpleton with a moustache incipient on a loose upper lip, who was required to do odd jobs and clean shoes and yet was a pupil in the lowest class – to us he looked about twenty-six. He was teased a lot, despite his being about 6 ft 4 in, or so it seemed to us. In an Eton suit he looked rather like a snow-capped Matterhorn on a winter's day.

Almost any feature, however undistinguished, of the house and grounds could be pressed into service and made to rank as a boon. The approach to many schools was through gates off the main road and past a lodge ('A resident gardener ensures plentiful supplies of fresh vegetables and fruit'), the gates being set in a wooded boundary-line. This thirty-yard-wide swath of tangled trees, shrubs, undergrowth and nettles is turned to great advantage: 'The extensive grounds include a handsome acreage of wild woodland, a favourite haunt of budding biologists, specimen-tins at the ready, not to speak of our lepidopterists and keen bug-hunters.' The last-named caused fearful trouble at Elmley when the headmaster was horrified to discover that the word's three syllables were being innocently contracted to two. Disconcerting to find that a local spinney is being referred to as 'a buggers' paradise'.

7.15 a.m.

High on the list of desirable items in a school's prospectus was a night porter. In the 1920s, when schools were full and wages were low, the number of unemployed ex-service men was large and the acquiring of a night porter was both easy and normal. 'Resident Night Porter' implied somebody in a constant state of vigilance throughout the long hours of darkness, an alert and sharp-eyed and -eared watchdog, a sort of scholastic Nana from *Peter Pan*, who patrolled the corridors and was ready to leap at and douse the flames that sometimes engulfed schools (parents with long memories could recall the terrible fire in a boys' house at Eton when barred windows had prevented the victims from escaping).

At my own prep school, the night porter's name was, appropriately, Knight. He was known to us as 'Mr Knight' in order to inculcate respect for our elders, irrespective of class, and the presence of a camp bed in the boiler room revealed his state of vigilance. But doubtless he would, in the event of a conflagration, have sprung to our assistance with one of those dusty and cone-shaped fire-fighting appliances ('Strike base sharply on floor and direct nozzle at seat of fire') that were strategically placed here and there. Provided one member of the staff gets damaged in a school

fire (PLUCKY PORTER BADLY BURNT) people feel comforted
that 'every effort was made'.

In my case our Mr Knight also undertook a disciplinary
role. Apart from the headmaster, his wife and the matrons,
no member of the staff lived in. There wasn't room for
them in those days when the school was chock-a-block
and it never crossed one's mind to wonder where they laid
their heads: presumably in some 'furnished rooms' in the
town. Therefore the maintenance of order prior to and
after Lights Out devolved upon the dormitory captain (a
feeble presence who just shouted 'Shut up' at intervals),
the matron on duty and Mr Knight, the headmaster being
busily occupied with cocktails and dinner and night caps
and work and more nightcaps and writing letters to
prospective parents ('I think I may say that we are a happy
school and Desmond should soon find his feet. The school
doctor is quite accustomed to tackling his little medical
trouble and I can assure you that here there is no stigma
attached to enuresis'.).

The duties of a night porter were various. He rang bells,
stoked boilers, tidied bathrooms, cleaned outdoor shoes,
and carried coals to the classrooms. He usually lived in some
basement room, had meals with the maids, got tips from
leavers (in the 1920s 2s 6d was the going rate) and sometimes achieved a mention in the headmaster's determinedly
jocular end-of-term speech: '. . . and during the cold snap,
I just don't know where we would all have been without
our faithful Bob (loud applause). He kept us all warm and
helped us to "snap out of it" (laughter and groans).'

To talk after 'No more talking' had been said was a crime
and Mr Knight had sharp ears. His alarmingly sudden cry
of, 'Get out of bed all those who were talking' still rings in
the ears. The subsequent punishment was far from severe
and, though incomprehensible and mysterious at the time,

these enlightened days seem now to offer a solution. Those of us who got caught were told to put on our dressing-gowns (brown woollen ones from Jaeger) and were marched from the dorm along to the headmaster's study where, in an atmosphere excitingly rich with cigar smoke and whisky fumes, we were told to take off our dressing-gowns and kneel, pyjama-clad, facing the wall and on a sort of long, padded hassock reminiscent of the communion rail in church. Did we look like a row of penitent choir-boys? Perhaps that was the trouble. We looked, and were, in-nocent, and maybe that was it. At all events, the headmaster, a rather lonely man whose wife seemed to have transferred her affections and emotional needs to her troop of Buff Orpingtons, scratched on for a time at his letters ('How pleasant and unusual in a boy to hear that your Humphrey takes such an interest in horticulture. He will find many an outlet here . . .') But then the pen was laid down and silence fell, a silence sometimes broken by weird, soft sounds, a mixture of accelerated breathing and clothing moving and the chair creaking. We referred to these as 'funny noises'. 'Whatever were those funny noises?' we said to each other as, released at last ('Off you go, boys!') we flocked back to 'Kitchener'. It never occurred to any of us, as we faced the wall and listened, to turn swiftly round and have a peep ('Oh my goodness!') at what was going on, if anything was.

In schools which did not boast a night porter, the task of ringing the awakening bell often fell to one of the under-matrons. Picture the dismay, therefore, of the headmaster of a Cumbrian school long since disbanded who, on hearing no bell, dispatched his wife to discover what had gone wrong and why Miss Binstead had 'let us all down'. Receiving no answer to her knock, the lady entered Miss Binstead's room to find her sleeping peacefully, tucked cosily up in bed with two thirteen-year-old boys who had recently, and understandably, failed their Common Entrance Exam. Alas, the spirited dialogue that must have followed this really very unusual discovery is not recorded (can the headmaster's wife have fired off with, 'What is the meaning of this?') but my informant tells me that Miss Binstead left the school on the next available train and the boys were, characteristically, allowed to stay on and take the Common Entrance Exam all over again. Headmasters, in their termly reports, are adept at skating lightly over unfortunate happenings – no point in making too much of a song and dance about it – and I dare say that these sexual pioneers' reports merely contained some such phrase as 'The term has not been without its faults.' An interesting point to note: the rest of the school could not apparently decide whether the two culprits were sissies for going anywhere near girls, or whether they were in fact frightfully grown up. You'll want to know about that Exam: yes, they both passed.

The getting-up bell gave an opportunity for a matron or the master on duty to count heads and make sure that all were present and correct. Boys who ran away seldom did so during the hours of darkness (after lunch seemed to be the preferred time). It was unusual for members of the staff to run away. They were assumed to be, like the baths and electric wiring, fixtures, but such departures have been known. I am told of a youngish Sussex matron who had been looking 'broody' for some weeks and 'not herself at all'. It seems that she had formed an unfortunate attachment in the shape of a local garage hand, a manly fellow who visited her frequently in her room, treated her to bottle after bottle of cooking sherry and was said to linger late. Matron got broodier by the day. She took to chain-smoking, played her gramophone till all hours, and one thrilling night the

dormitories were awoken by the loud splutter of a motor-
bicycle on the gravel drive outside. Rushing hastily to the
windows, the boys could just make out in the dim light
matron perched on the pillion and being then whisked
away to Paradise down the Petworth road (is it remembered
that Barbara Cartland once wrote a novel entitled *Love
Rides Pillion*? This incident may well have been the
inspiration). Her luggage, neatly packed and labelled, was
found next day in her room with a notice on it saying KINDLY
FORWARD. The under-matron took over when her senior's
scholastic career had ceased upon the midnight with no
pain, save that of the boys awaiting medical attention next
day, and although no overt reference was ever made to
matron's absence, the headmaster, in that obligatory end-
of-term speech, did say, in the well-worn phrase, 'The term
has not been without incident.' But that might refer to
anything – the startling 7–1 win over Westfield Court, the
minor 'flu epidemic, the school play (*Toad of Toad Hall*)
or the lecture by Canon Slowly-Jones on 'Numismatics for
Beginners'.

At my school, Stirling Court, there was another motor-
bicycle elopement but of a rather different kind. In this
case the motor-bicycle had a side-car and the male part of
the affair was a member of our staff, a rather pungently
scented rotundity who taught Latin and made eyes at the
maids who, flattered by this unusual compliment, made
eyes back, dangerous though it was ('Tell Wheeler I want
to see her after lunch'). Whence had this third-rate creature
come and what his credentials? Some schools had to take
what they could get and it was well known that the scholastic agents, Chitty and Gale, naturally made the very best
of the material that they were asked to place. Thus, somebody who in younger days and merely as a matter of routine,
had at school been 'confirmed', became at once 'a devout

communicant who would, we are sure, be prepared to tackle religious instruction to senior forms'. A grudging word of praise from a previous employer is, 'He comes with a fine reputation.' I dare say that even a spell in gaol would be transmogrified into 'Widely experienced; some of his time has been spent in other fields.'

Evidently short of cash, the master in question confiscated, on the flimsiest grounds, our pens and penknives and a few watches, pawned them in Gosport and then left by motor-bicycle, also on the midnight, with a chorus girl from the pierrot troop in 'Hello Hampshire!' on the pier, evidently a conscientious girl mindful of her public, for she had duly made her twice-nightly stage appearance before joining her lover in his motorized *char de Vénus*. As usual, there was no official reference to the matter and Latin was abandoned for the rest of the term, but we learnt the full details from our Mr Knight, a willing gas-bag. And for a year or two and as with an absconding cashier, various sightings of the Latinist were reported. He had been seen in Brighton. He had been seen in Hereford. Parents had spotted him at Gleneagles and, most improbable of all, on the Blue Train. Our penknives must have been more valuable than we imagined.

Although it was unusual for members of the staff to run away, it was rarer still for prep school boys to make a successful get-away. Statistics are hard to come by, for a confession about unofficial absentees doesn't look well, but it is clear that boys have run away from their public schools in far larger numbers and with a higher success rate than those at prep schools. The reasons are obvious – they are older, they have less supervision, they have money for fares, they often have access to bicycles for that first leg to Bletchley, they can look up bus and train times and, having been at school so much longer, the urge to go is sharper.

I had a friend – killed, alas, in the war while doing immensely brave low-level bombing – who must, I think, hold the record (six times in a year) for hooking it from Winchester. He chose different times of day and cleverly varied his route up to Cheshire until the day when the college understandably lost patience and he was allowed to run away for ever. And there is a pleasing story told of Wellington where a housemaster, returning to his house for lunch, was told that a parent awaited him in his study. It was a mother, and she rose, white-faced, to her feet. 'I've brought Douglas back,' she said. '*Back*?' 'Yes, and he is very sorry for what he has done.' The boy had run away the night before, and not a soul had noticed it.

An attempted escape from, of all happy schools, Summer Fields, is on record.

I tried to run away once. With a friend, I intended to reach the station and, hiding under the seat of a train, reach London, where a relative was staying. The execution wasn't bad, as far as it went (the Broad, in Oxford). At tea that evening we each stowed a slice of bread and butter in our pockets in case we felt hungry during the journey and then, when the rest of the school lined up in the corridor for chapel, we slipped into the coat-room. Nobody missed us and, when everyone else had marched away, we walked out through the masters' door past the gym. We each had with us a golf club – not as weapons, but because they happened to be our most prized possessions and, as I say, we tramped as far as the Broad. Here we got lost, because I couldn't remember the way to the station and, finally, we went up to a taxi-driver and asked him to take us there. When he seemed suspicious, we said that our uncle had died and we had to get to London. He still seemed suspicious. We offered him our school tiepins and even our golf clubs as fare, but it became plainer and plainer that he was unconvinced. Finally, he asked us if we came from Summer Fields or the Dragon and, somewhat stunned by his perspicacity, we admitted all. He took us back and we each got four of the best.

Why did they try to escape? Our informant, who is the son of Dornford Yates, adds inconsequentially that 'the five years at Summer Fields were the happiest of my boyhood'.

Fifty years ago, a boy's first act on being woken by the bell would have been to get out of bed and continue filling the chamber-pot which, on retiring the night before, he had begun to fill. These unsavoury and unhygienic contraptions were necessary when, at bedtime and with the door to the outside lavatories locked, there were usually only a couple of indoor lavatories available for seventy or so boys and these were reserved, by common consent, for boys requiring to achieve what was then known to young people as No. 2. What No. 1 was speaks for itself. The chamber-pots were subsequently emptied by the maids (and damp patches on the floor occasionally indicated that it was an act needing skill) into enamel slop-pails, a depressing word for a depressing object. At one school of my acquaintance, a boy, larking about, broke a chamber-pot and wondered, for all breakages were firmly charged up on the end-of-term account, how the damaged item might, in those prudish days, appear. But the authorities rose to the challenge and claimed their rights with the words 'Large tea-cup . . . 5s.'

In some schools cold baths were, in winter as in summer,

compulsory, and in one case were personally supervised by
the headmaster, wisely clad in his macintosh.

> Three baths stood next to each other, each one
> filled nearly to the brim with cold water, so that the
> displacement of a small boy would bring the water
> level up to the brim. It was forbidden to spill a
> drop of water over the back end of the bath in
> the course of lying down, so that one was forced
> to lean back very slowly and finally to remain
> lying down for approximately three to five seconds.
> The act of getting out also had to be conducted in
> such a way that as little water was spilled as pos-
> sible. Only sickness or the granting of a privileged
> state excused the morning bath.

The business of dressing for breakfast had to be accomplished with care, for in many schools there was a mysterious
code of conduct involved. Although on bath nights the
boys undressed completely and unselfconsciously, washed
themselves and splashed each other and larked about,
naked and the picture of innocence, the business of dressing
in the morning and undressing at night had to be accomplished without the slightest display of what were usually
called Private Parts. Parts that, for communal baths, could
be entirely public and remained unremarked on, must, at
other times, be totally private and concealed. Vests and
shirts must go on before pyjama trousers could be lowered
and discarded. Pants, and this could be a tricky moment,
must be carefully slipped up into place under the shirt,
after which you were fairly safe. Negligence in the matter
was referred to as 'showing sights' and anybody observing
a carelessly displayed private part was at liberty to shout
'Sights!', adding the name of the culprit. The game of

'Beaver', popular at the period, made everybody alert and ready to shout. Seeing a bearded man in the street and being the first to shout 'Beaver', you scored a point (what a time players of the game would have in our present hirsute era).

Details exist of what was, in the nineteenth century, considered to be the minimum requirement in the way of a school's domestic staff.

> Finally, the domestic staff is worth enumerating, if only to make a twentieth-century headmaster's imagination boggle; a lady superintendent, two nurses, a governess, a cook-housekeeper, a cook, two nursemaids, a parlourmaid, six housemaids, two lady's maids, a wardrobe maid, a wardrobe woman (a subtle social distinction), a schoolroom maid, a dining-room maid, a kitchen maid, a scullery maid, a butler, two footmen, two coachmen, a groom; and an unspecified number of gardeners, one of whom slept in an attic over the toolshed.

In the pre-war days when housemaids were still freely available, they were often housed in the attics of the main house and where the headmaster's wife could keep an eye on them. They were usually called by their surnames (Parker, Bishop, Cooper) and shared their accommodation with the 'working' cook, an adjective that removed her for ever from polite society and rated a much lower salary than a 'lady' cook, the latter being a quite recent innovation in the scholastic and culinary world and demanding such exotic things as a wireless set and her own room and an electric kettle and invitations to tea.

The maids, when they existed, rose at 6.30, washed themselves in hand basins, dressed and then clattered,

probably in the resentful manner to which they were fully entitled, down the back stairs to lend a hand with the preparations for breakfast. The kitchen was often adjacent to the dining-room and had a hatch through which the cook could occasionally be dimly glimpsed and who, against a steamy and watery background, looked, in her white overall, not unlike a spectral visitor, a spirit Called from the Vasty Deep, a call that, from the look on her face, had failed to please her.

Cooking smells often reached the dormitories and alerted
the boys to what was awaiting them as their main *plat* and
a smell of fish sometimes meant that the cook was lavishing
her artistry on some sections of smoked haddock left over
from the supper before last and now to be deftly trans-
formed into kedgeree (egg and bacon for the masters), the
fishy aroma being greeted by every boy with the word 'Poo!',
the more histrionic boys holding their noses and making
faces.

It is a scene that many will remember. The kedgeree
stands ready on the hot plate. The maids stand ready to
hand round the plates when the masters have, in a fine
fishy fragrance, served it out. The porridge has already
been ladled out and is rapidly congealing on the plates.
The warm milk and the sugar, one spoonful per boy,
awaits. Parker has set off through the baize door for the
Private Side (headmasters' wives seldom appear so early)
bearing grilled sausages and scrambled eggs. Grace has
been delivered ('Bless, oh Lord, this food to our use and us
to thy service') and everybody has sat down, and in no time
at all a boy, possibly unnerved by an earlier shout of
'Sights!', has spilt the milk on the table-cloth and has had
to rise from his seat, a trying experience at that age, and
walk to where the Fine List hangs on the wall. There he
writes down his name and details of the incident: 'Baxter.
Milk. 1d.' Gravy is 2d.

The headmaster naturally presides at the feast, seated at
a separate table, and this is perhaps the right moment for
taking a look at those in this most responsible and worrying
office.

8 a.m.

Headmasters were largely what is known as laws unto themselves. Unlimited power did not necessarily and invariably corrupt, though there are instances of corruption: it merely allowed those who possessed oddities to give such oddities fullest rein. For instance, 'One curious rule of the school was that it was obligatory to go in the company of the Headmaster to the Ascot Races on the Heath,' a rule which many would be delighted to obey. Well then, what about this?

> At our school the head had a bathroom built in one corner of a classroom, no one knew why. He used to sit on the edge of the bath, fully clothed and reading 'Whodunnits', and at certain irregular times the door would open and he would emerge still reading and then disappear out of the other end of the classroom like a sleepwalking Lady Macbeth.

And another headmaster, abandoning temporarily the classroom, took time off to run a profitable commercial side-line:

> As I mentioned, most of the local population were fishermen and as their living gradually declined with·the silting up of the estuary, our head, on

taking over the school, opened up a factory at the
end of the promenade for potting shrimps which he
sold to the public. As a result there was the remarkable sight of the headmaster going round the
dining-room, as the boys were having tea, wearing
a hat and carrying a pedler's basket from which he
sold them potted shrimps.

One schoolmaster, applying for a post, had the unnerving
experience of watching his prospective employer fall
asleep during his interview. Applicants elsewhere had
equally trying experiences:

'Spell Eleemosynary.' These were the first words
ever spoken to me by the headmaster of a well
known prep school in Cheshire, to which I had
journeyed on a bleak November afternoon to
discuss the possibility of my joining the school to
teach Mathematics. I arrived about 4 p.m. and
was announced in a large room with a long oval
table round which many people were still lingering
over lunch. As I entered, I noticed an elderly man
sitting at the far end. A hand shot out with finger
pointing. 'Spell Eleemosynary.' Only mildly surprised, as I had already met several eccentric
heads, I complied. 'Good, spell committee.' I did
so, but feeling there was some little misunder-
standing, perhaps. I diffidently mentioned that my
subject was Mathematics. 'Damn Mathematics,
spell fuschia.' 'Good,' said he, 'don't go back to
Sheffield (where I was then teaching), join us now
and I'll send for all your goods.' Of course this was
quite impracticable, but I agreed to join the following term. The school was very well equipped, with

a large outdoor swimming-bath and also a small theatre of which I was promised sole command.

And so began ten most exciting, sometimes hilarious, years of my life.

It was in no way unusual for a headmaster to parade his own political beliefs before the school and imply that such beliefs were the only possible ones to have. At my own prep school, any boy failing to support the Conservative Cause would have been viewed with suspicion and very probably punished in some oblique way.

The headmaster was a virulent politician and a fanatical Tory. On the 5th of November an effigy of Mr Gladstone used to be burnt in the grounds, and there was a little note in the Gazette to say there were only seven Liberals in the school, the least of whom was myself. One day somebody rashly sent the head a Liberal circular. He sent it back with some coppers inside, so that the recipient should have to pay eightpence on receipt of it, and the whole school was told of his action. One day there was a by-election going on hard-by. All the school were taken with blue ribbons on their jackets except the unfortunate seven Liberals, who were told to stay at home and work.

And as time went on, worse than Liberals appeared:

I was still at Belmont in 1926 when the General Strike took place. Like most prep schools Belmont was 'true blue' and Tory, so that the strikers were considered to be 'Bolshies' or 'Reds'. There was in fact a suspicion that all working class people were 'Reds'. We had a boy, only one, whose parents were socialists. The headmaster did not hesitate to give us all a lecture in front of this wretched boy, pointing out how unpatriotic it was to support the strikers, and from that moment he found himself completely shunned by all the little sons of die-hard conservatives. Many years later one of Clement Attlee's sons appeared as a pupil at Belmont!

When I was about thirteen I announced at home that I was a Liberal. This caused consternation in the family, because one was expected to be a Conservative regardless of age. But I had once sat on Lloyd-George's knee, and had just finished his war memoirs, so I was determined to be a Liberal . . . and have remained one ever since.

Many of those who went to prep schools in the early 1920s and with the First World War still a terrible memory, will recall a staff of demobilized misfits, unsuited for the scholastic world and struggling to earn a living in the 'country fit for heroes to live in':

For the 'old man' as we somewhat unoriginally called him, was a social misfit. That he could be permitted to set up as a practitioner in education was an anomaly in the national outlook, a kind of liability to balance the books and to help pay for the merits of the free enterprise system. His background: a late Victorian upbringing in Scotland, a well known public school (one of the top twelve), Cambridge and the Army. Nostalgically (perhaps) he retained his military rank, a practice that nowadays seems so quaint. He was badly gassed in the 1914–18 war, for which tragedy we had nothing but sympathy. It undoubtedly, however, affected his whole outlook and may well have accounted for the ungovernable outbursts of temper to which he was prone.

There was nothing more terrifying for us to experience than one of 'the old man's blowings-up'. Generally they were entirely unpredictable and almost always took place when he was either carving in the dining room or vulgarly munching a chop, the gravy clinging to his abundant moustache and dripping down his chin. Something would set him off, a harmless remark from a boy sitting near, or an innocent youthful gesture; he would flush and address himself to the offender, his voice getting louder and louder till he was shouting and trembling with rage. The whole room, mesmerized by this performance, would sit hushed – boys, masters, mistresses, matrons, maids. For a full minute or two it would go on, a tirade of invective and opprobrium; then, exhausted, he would continue carving or munching his chop. Invariably, however, he would be guilt-stricken, for after the meal he would take the boy aside and say, 'Put your pads on; I'll bowl to you in the nets.'

Catapults would now appear to be a thing of the past but at one time they featured prominently in school life and provided yet another instance of unpredictability. One would think that these potentially dangerous weapons would be in no way encouraged, but Maurice Baring reports that, 'Catapults were permitted, and indeed shot and elastic were supplied by the school at a reduced price, and one day Swinburne mi. was shot in the back of the neck by Shelley.' Even stranger was what went on at St Andrew's, Eastbourne:

Life for the boys under E.L.B. was something of a
gamble. They found him disturbingly unpredictable. He was just as capable of displaying
unexpected gentleness and kindness as he was of
indulging in what seemed to them unbridled
savagery. His reaction to a catapult 'craze' illustrates E.L.B.'s unpredictability, his overgrown
childishness, his love of shooting and his ability to
take a potential 'nuisance' and 'organize' it. Unlike
most adults before and since, E.L.B. approved of
catapults, because they fostered 'co-ordination of
hand and eye'—a favourite theme of his—but he, like
the cows on the way to Herstmonceux, realized
that they were dangerous weapons. E.L.B. suddenly surprised the school by decreeing that every
boy should have a catapult. The materials necessary
for making it would be supplied, but everyone had
to cut his own catapult fork from a suitable tree. A
few boys got their mothers to send them catapults
from Harrods; very glossy, they had varnished
handles and metal forks. They were promptly
seized and confiscated by E.L.B., and the luckless
boys were scornfully told to produce home-made
catapults within two days. All the boys were provided with permits from the Chief Constable to
have and to use catapults. To encourage proficient
shooting, targets were set up on the asphalt playground; Blogg made them with planks and sand-
bags, and with 'ricochet-stops' at each wing. These
were the only legitimate targets, but there were
those who took to peppering the hindquarters of
cab-horses making their weary way up the hill, or
shooting at the glass-sided flagpole-tower on the top
of the school. They were suitably rewarded by

E.L.B. One Sunday some boys took a supply of bread from the dining-room at breakfast and after chapel they went up to the cubicles; they threw the bread on to the flat roof outside the windows, and waited for sparrows. As their salvoes were being discharged they realized that standing behind them was E.L.B. They awaited the awful wrath. With a twinkle in his eye he said, 'Quite a Judas' feast,' and walked away. The boys fled.

In addition to catapults, a schoolboy's armoury contained another effective weapon:

Once I should obviously have been given the sack when, after taking the cricket XI in a brake to Cothill, on our return we found a police sergeant awaiting us at the boarding house, and with him a rubicund gentleman with a bandaged eye who complained that we had all shot at him with pea-shooters when crossing Folly Bridge.

Subsequent legend has discarded the suggestion of collective responsibility, making the skipper himself the successful marksman, elated by a Dragon victory and using a pea-shooter confiscated with a stern rebuke on the outward journey.

Dual-headmasters and, as we shall see, headmistresses, were by no means a rarity, doubtless in the spirit of a trouble shared is a trouble halved.

Foxy looks fierce but he is very decent really. He always ties his tie in a big knot and wears plus-fours. He plays golf a lot and did something brave in the Great War. I asked him if he had ever seen the Angel of Mons, and he just laughed. It's the opposite with old Apps (he's the other headmaster). He looks very kind, but he isn't really – nor is his wife though she is very pi. She plays the piano for prayers every night in a long brown dress. She looks very hard at the music and has a drip on the end of her long nose. Every morning when old Apps takes roll-call, he starts off, 'Good evening, gentlemen – and others.' I laughed about the first half a dozen times. Now I have given up because I know he counts me among the 'others'. When Apps swishes he really hurts, but Foxy only gives one a tap or two. Perhaps it is because after being in the war he doesn't want to inflict any more pain. I bet old Apps never went near the war.

And from Somerset there came, complete with wives, a rather more sedate pair:

The Harrison brothers, Wilfred was tall, spidery and classical, Aelfric tweedy, sports-mad, but also versed in the classics. Both had apparently played cricket for the county, the latter batting with his right arm only, the left one having been shattered in the war. But in spite of incessant sporting activities, they were kind men. If there is much sadness in prep schools, blame the parents for sending their children; the Harrisons did all they could to make life bearable.

Their wives? Very much in the background. Wilfred's wife sometimes prowled through the dormitories, always after lights out, wearing a pair of old slippers which announced themselves a long way off, but she never spoke and was a rather ghostly visitor. Aelfric's wife had a cork leg which played her up in warm weather, so she could not do much prowling. She worried a lot about her daughter, Sheila, who was for ever 'running a fever'. Sheila took her lessons and her walks with the boys and on one occasion I threw a cowpat at her.

Ordained headmasters are now seldom seen and past experience of them has not always left a warm glow behind.

At the age of nine I was sent to a Jesuit prep school in the South of England. The school was presided over by a devout priest who somehow seems on reflection to have been too distant from the boys.

He was assisted by a spiteful old priest who liked to show off his biceps and talk about Roman bravery in the Punic wars and Protestant hooligans getting hit with policemen's truncheons. He disliked me personally and encouraged other boys to shun my company. The remainder of the staff consisted of three non-ordained Jesuits (they are now all priests). One, a kind of music hall sergeant-major, had a face like a giraffe and roared a lot at the boys while boasting of his severity in former years; the second had a sort of pimply gargoyle face and a bad temper, often punishing boys unreasonably; the third was a kind of ecclesiastical sportsmaster.

Punishment was severe, the instrument used being a loaded tawse called a 'ferula' and getting oneself beaten was all too easy. There was a proliferation of rules and permission had. to be obtained for almost every human activity, including going to the toilet, which was called the 'commonplace'. Nervous boys occasionally fouled their trousers to the great amusement of the others, who tormented them persistently and refused to let them live it down. Indeed the boys were the cruellest and most spiteful body of human beings I have ever known, their favourite pleasure seeming to be to reduce their fellow pupils to tears. They were, however, great animal lovers and, when letters arrived from home, photographs of puppies, kittens and ponies were shown round with great enthusiasm. But boys of dark-skinned or foreign appearance were disliked equally by the masters and the other boys, as were those with non-upper class accents.

Religion was enforced, naturally, and there were sermons on the 'wickedness of the Bolsheviks', which only served to make me regard the Russians with a measurement of approval right up to the Nazi-Soviet pact of 1939. I have not, however, abandoned my own religious practice, or my hatred of cruelty.

Public humiliation as an effective method of punishment was all too common among headmasters:

> Mr Evans had some quaint ideas about discipline. In a corner of the dining-room was a bare table with a framed picture of a large pig hanging above it. This was the school Pig Table, a place of punishment visible to everyone, with two bare forms and room for about six boys. During each week we collected 'Black Marks' for any misdemeanours, however trivial, and all these crimes were recorded in a 'Black Mark Book'. For instance:
>
> Slacking during cricket practice.
>
> > Montgomery mi.   2 marks.
>
> Taking a short cut on a run.
>
> > Montgomery mi.   3 marks.
>
> All entries were read out to the whole school once a week, a devastating experience for small boys of six to eight, and if a boy accumulated ten marks, he was sent to the 'Pig Table' for a week, which meant that all his meals were second-rate, with margarine instead of butter, smaller helpings and special punishment dishes; no sugar, cakes, jam or treacle. As I was often at the 'Pig Table' I frequently had to bribe friends to hide food for me to supplement the meagre ration.

But now to our headmistresses:

> I have vivid recollections of the two sisters, both maiden ladies, who ran a small prep school in

Worcestershire, fifty years ago. The elder was dark, slight, pale and severe, with a permanent frown induced by her pince-nez; I don't remember seeing her smile. The younger was fair and comely with a discontented expression, and looked as if she could smile, but preferred not to. The elder invariably wore black, the younger occasionally a light-coloured blouse. We feared them both equally, though I now think that they cannot have been as grim as we imagined them.

The only occasion when they became at all human was when we did well at games. On the other hand, dropped catches at cricket, or slacking at football seemed to make them positively dislike us. Once, when we returned defeated from a soccer match, the elder principal took us all into a classroom and wrote on the blackboard: WHY SCHOOL LOST THE MATCH (heavily underlined) and dictated twelve reasons. Number one was 'Too much brotherly love.' Alas, I cannot remember the other reasons, but the first was so odd that I have never forgotten it.

And so to another headmistress, in this case operating on her own:

The school was then run by the widow of its founder, a formidable looking soul who seldom spoke to us but ruled through a headmaster and a couple of male assistants, all graduates, plus two unqualified but hefty daughters. In a large house with tatty outbuildings, an asphalted playground and a mown paddock, some seventy day boys and five boarders were 'prepared' for something, mostly for public schools, Common Entrance successes being acclaimed from time to time at morning prayers. The rare scholarship or exhibition won by some brainy swot overcame our loathing of him by bringing us a half-holiday by way of celebration of his success. The regular Wednesday and Saturday halfdays were sacred to games, watched and cheered by the non-players.

One of the hefty daughters did three things for me; reported to my parents that I could not see the blackboard (leading to spectacles, rare and derisory among children, but with blessed dispensation from those literally bloody games); savaged me verbally for sneaking to her about another boy, and physically for cocking a snook at the Union Jack when we were supposed to be saluting it on Empire Day.

The quality in boys at which all headmasters aimed, or in some enlightened cases pretended to aim, was that which is called 'manliness', that quality so highly prized in many of the books (Sapper, Buchan, Henty) and magazines (The B.O.P., Chums) that were read by schoolboys, 'manliness' being in itself an amalgam of courage and decency and dignity and nobility and putting your best foot forward (the left foot, in the case of cricket and of right-handed players). It was manly to take hard knocks without blubbing. It was manly to stop runaway horses, the supply of which was, in some areas, a bit limited. It was manly to 'own up' to a misdeed that was going to end in corporal punishment. It was manly to protect women, though the only women to be seen were matron, usually a formidable person in no sort of need of protection, and the headmaster's wife, frequently invisible behind her baize door. And it was very manly to be good at games.

The following poem, printed some years ago in a school magazine, reveals, although in exaggerated terms, what was once, and perhaps is still in some quarters, the general opinion of and attitude to a non-games-player – the muff or softy, to give the wretched boy no harsher name.

THE FEMININE BOY

If cursed by a son who declined to play cricket
   (Supposing him sound and sufficient in thews),
I'd larrup him well with the third of a wicket,
   Selecting safe parts of his body to bruise.
In his mind such an urchin King Solomon had
When he said, 'Spare the stump, and you bungle
                     the lad!'

For what in the world is the use of a creature
   All flabbily bent on avoiding the pitch?
Who wanders about, with a sob in each feature,
   Devising a headache, inventing a stitch?
There surely would be a quick end to my joy
If possessed of that monster – the feminine boy!

The feminine boy who declines upon croquet,
   Or halma, or spillikins (horrible sport!),
Or any amusement that's female and pokey,
   And flatly objects to behave as he ought!
I know him of old. He is lazy and fat,
And sadly in need of the thick of a bat!

Instead of this Thing, fit for punishment drastic,
   Give, Fortune, a son who is nimble and keen;
A bright-hearted sample of human elastic,
   As fast as an antelope, supple and clean;
Far other than he in whose dimples there lodge
Significant signs of inordinate stodge.

Ay, give me the lad who is eager and chubby,
   A Stoddart in little, a hero in bud;
Who'd think it a positive crime to grow stubby,
   And dreams half the night he's a Steel or a Studd!
There's the youth for my fancy, all youngsters above,
The boy for my handshake, the lad for my love!

And manliness could show itself, as a fond mother informs us, even in such minor matters as pyjama buttons.

> I learnt about four years after it happened that he ('Humph') was beaten on his second night – he was in a dormitory with two second-year boys and one who had been there longer. Everyone got beaten. Also on the first night the head went round the dorms and Humph had his pyjama jacket buttoned up to the top, quite primly. 'Be sporting,' said the head and undid the pyjama top button. So that was one of the things.

Headmasters often considered it their duty to attempt to acquaint the more senior boys, then aged a good old twelve or thirteen, with what are known as the facts of life, and here the track record of headmasters is a truly deplorable one.

> Mr Gibbs (did he ever possess a Christian name?) of Gibbs Preparatory School, Sloane Street, used to have a private talk with individual leavers which we presumed would be mutually embarrassing, but turned out to be a homily on evacuating the bowels thrice daily. 'Look at me,' he would say; we looked at him. 'I always go to the lavatory three times a day.' We waited for what was bound to follow, assuming that this was the overture to more serious

matters, but he had lost interest in us and we tip-toed softly from the presence.

And even when reliance was placed on the printed word, nothing very sensational was achieved.

It was in the study that boys due to leave read a pamphlet which was much talked about, and which gave them their official sex instruction before they moved on to the horrors of the sophisticated public school world. The dire consequences of 'solitary vice' were touched upon, but the book was a disappointment. It was shrouded in as much mystery as Pandora's Box, but nothing good or evil seemed to fly out of it. Birds and bees flitted across the pages, but it really cleared up none of the often-discussed, highly inaccurate theories of the origins of life. Nor did E.L.B.'s Talk. He made vague references to 'certain parts of your body which are given to you for use only when you are married'. He followed this by the puzzling admonition 'never to do anything which might cause pain or sorrow to your sister'. There were further incomprehensible mutterings, again about birds and bees, and that was that.

Not a single correspondent has come forward to claim that he was on the receiving end of clear and concise information. Not a single soul, it seems, pressed on to his public school fully informed.

I well recall the glad day, at my own Hampshire prep school, when it was clear that the answer to the sexual riddle was to be given us. All the boys in the top form were summoned to the headmaster's study and we all feared that some giant misdemeanour had been discovered and that we were about to be beaten. Not at all. The headmaster, whom we all liked, was looking geniality itself and invited us, a previously unknown politeness, to sit down. It was plain to the dimmest boys what was in the wind.

'Ah, what a dusty answer gets the soul,' wrote Meredith, 'when hot for certainties in this our life!' and no answers could compete in dustiness with those that were then given us. Hot for certainties we certainly were, and no more dirty-minded, I suppose, than the average boy of our age and era.

'I expect you've all been wondering how you got here,' he said. 'Well, it's like this. When two people love one another, there's this little thing that's provided by the gentleman, and there's this little thing that's provided by the lady, and they both meet in the lady's cave and form a baby. Now, are there any questions?'

We were, of course, full of questions but nobody dared to ask them. We emerged as baffled and ill-informed as we went in. And even at my public school, no clear facts were ever given; and here was a rum thing. Whenever the subject of 'love' appeared, those in authority looked both disapproving and panic-stricken. It seemed strange that a subject so highly considered both in poetry and in literature should be so productive of worried looks and dire warnings.

Smutty talk, too, caused considerable anxiety, opinions being always sharply divided as to what ranked as smut and what didn't. Roughly speaking, if you were in any doubt, it was smut.

Nowadays there is much controversy over sex instruction in schools, just as if it was something new. Forty years ago the leaving boys were all assembled and the headmaster began the proceedings with prayer. We were then given the authentic birds and bees story, with much talk, all veiled in allegory. There was a dread note of forsakement by God if we did certain things (unspecified); and warnings of Torquemadic agonies if we fell into various (unspecified) temptations. No diagrams were drawn; no biological or physiological terms were used. After further prayer, we were cast into the outer darkness of our pubescent doubts, and stood about on the gravel, gazing upon each other with a wild surmise. That was all. Our fathers were, of course, delighted to receive, during the holidays, a letter apologizing for usurping parental privilege, but indicating that Philip was now fully informed on the significance of his coming manhood, and could enter the wider world etc etc . . .

Smut standards varied from school to school, and era to era.

'Words which you wouldn't like your mother or your sisters to hear' called for strict disciplinary measures. Boys were encouraged by E.L.B. to 'sneak' on one another for this misdemeanour. One unfortunate was betrayed for using the word 'bum', and was called to the study where he was birched on the bare buttocks until he bled. This episode illustrates, in more than one respect, the worst in E.L.B.'s Victorianism.

8.15 a.m.

In memories of school food it is delightful to find universal reverence paid to the humble sausage. Even wartime sausages, containing heaven knows what, were very highly rated as comestibles.

Graham Robertson, while strongly challenging the view that his days at his prep school were the happiest of his life, does speak in the most glowing terms of Thursday morning, for on Thursday it was Sausage Morning and even as far off as Tuesday he began to be 'filled with a vague joy' at the prospect. There were insufficient sausages (they could be heard excitingly 'fizzling' as they were carried in) to provide a second one for each boy and so the surplus ones were doled out according to the boys' precedence in class. Could there be a finer incentive to work hard, and in consequence and during his first term, Mr Robertson took three prizes and if the term lasted twelve weeks, a dozen extra sausages.

An over-fondness for sausages, however, could bring trouble with it.

I remember one curious episode happening. One of the masters found a letter addressed to one of the boys written to him by another boy. This was the

text of the letter: 'Dear Mister C., – May I have my sausage next Sunday at breakfast because I am very hungry.'

'Mr C.,' it was discovered, had been regularly levying a tribute from his neighbour at breakfast for some weeks, and the other boy, a much smaller boy, had had to go without his sausage. 'Mr C.' was severely flogged in front of the whole school.

And can it have been the Sunday sausage that produced the following surprise result?

Whether we were well fed according to modern standards or fussy mothers, I do not know. There was a certain dullness about the slabs of bread and butter for tea, but we had plenty to eat. I still have an affectionate regard for potted meat acquired at school, and sausages, on Sunday mornings I think, were delicious. I do not remember ever being ill there, though once when I came home for the holidays my grandmother remarked, 'You're looking very green and ugly.'

But sausages were not the only excitement, and here a word of praise over the years to the cook for managing to boil forty nutritious ovoids satisfactorily and at the same time, no easy feat.

THE DAY WE HAD AN EGG FOR BREAKFAST (the only time during my year and a bit at the school). This necessitated the school's entire population of forty or so boys being put to creating paper egg cups, as there were none of the real variety; as it was Eastertide we were required to paint the eggs with suitable decorations the day before. There were no hens on the premises so it remained a mystery as to what prompted this unusually beneficent gesture.

That reference to a boy looking very green and ugly brings us by a natural transition to a subject that agitated, and perhaps still does, the staffs, and especially the matrons, of prep schools, the subject being defecation, that daily and post-breakfast task that must, somehow or other, be accomplished successfully. The slightest sign of sluggishness was promptly dealt with. At Stirling Court every boy had a bi-termly dose of Gregory Powder, that name that sounded vaguely like the managing director of some City firm ('. . . I will now ask Sir Gregory to sum up.'). To those lucky few who lack experience of its explosive power and repellent colour (it looks all too like what it is aiming to produce), let me say that it is the aperient to end all aperients, ensuring hours of griping pain upon the lavatory seat. It was, later in the day, accompanied by merciless cross-questioning. 'Have you been?' was the less than lovely phrase in use. One assumes that this dread purgative was invented by a Dr Gregory, now dead. Is it too much to hope that, like the inventors of gun-powder and the guillotine, he perished by his own invention, preferably from an over-generous intake of powder?

Gregory Powder, however, had a rival.

I was at Orleton School, Scarborough from 1927–32. The headmaster and owner was a Mr Venables, but a relation, perhaps a sister or sister-in-law, a Mrs Cooper, was the main power in the school. Mrs Cooper was paranoic about all the boys being 'regular' at all times. To this end she insisted on everyone daily having a large spoonful of a laxative called 'Agaroll', which had an oily texture and tasted of bad fish. In the course of a year the boys consumed crates of Agaroll. Even after five years I never learned to tolerate this obnoxious concoction.

Treatment of illness amongst the boys in the school was simple, at least in the early stages. Whatever minor ailment one was sickening for the remedy was always the same – Agaroll.

The following is a fine example of really conscientious attention to bowel movements.

Immediately after breakfast the headmaster's wife would set herself up with a brown exercise book at a long table in the school hall. Each line of her book recorded the day-by-day bowel behaviour of the child whose name appeared in the left-hand margin. With a crisp briefing, 'Smith minor No 6' or 'Forbes-Hetherington No 10', the children were dispatched to the various School lavatories . . . His mission completed, each child would return to the command post and report, 'Yes, please,' or 'No, please,' depending on how successful he had been. She would then enter the result in the appropriate square, a '1' for 'yes' and a '0' for 'no'.

The system was hardly a success. If the boys were away too long, or not long enough, there would be a tightening of the lip and close interrogation. And if they replied 'no', they not only earned her obvious displeasure, but suffered retaliation – either liquid cascara or, for habitual sins of omission, castor oil. Under these circumstances, it is hardly surprising that they learned to say 'yes' rather than 'no'; nor, indeed, that many of them became more or less chronically constipated.

There was one other unfortunate by-product of these events – one which the headmaster's wife liked to call 'lavatory misdemeanours'. No doubt bored by having to wait the required period behind closed doors, the boys would while away their time with carving designs on the seat, dismantling the plumbing and, to use the headmaster's words, 'desecrating the toilet roll'; this usually took the form of pulling out the centre to make several yards of translucent paper telescope. The results of these peccadilloes were inevitably discovered by the headmaster's wife, whose pleasure it was to inspect the lavatories each day. Needless to say, retribution was swift and harsh. Indeed so harsh was the punishment, and so deep the disgrace into which the culprit was plunged, that few, if any, dared own up to their crimes. Under such circumstances the rule was that the whole should suffer for the sins of the individual, and the entire school would be detained.

In some schools, the steps taken to keep the machinery smoothly working were not quite so drastic and, if one may so phrase it, fundamental.

In 1926 my cousin and her husband started a prep school of their own at Aldwick, Bognor, to which I was moved. This was called Field Place and it was, more by design than accident, exactly the opposite of Belmont. At that time there was a movement in England called 'New Health', started (and profitably continued) by Sir William Arbuthnot Lane, who believed in bowel action, fresh fruit, dates, sunbathing, fresh air, nuts and Vita-sun windows (they let in ultra-violet rays). Plenty of roughage, he said, would keep the bowels active.

By and large the duty of defecation supervision devolved, as did so much else, on the school matron and under-matrons (the school average appears to be one matron to about twenty-five boys), those dedicated and kind and wholly indispensable persons who are here remembered in a variety of ways.

For their firmness:

> I remember being summoned by matron in front of the whole school and sent to bed in the middle of a Bulldog Drummond film, whose details are still etched on the memory, for not having brushed my teeth . . . and being told by an under-matron that my attitude towards Jews was un-Christian . . . (it was).

For their dispensing of tasty tonics:

> . . . Though to set against that, they didn't qualify for the malt parade in the morning. A good time this, with giant economy jars of Radio Malt and Keplers ranged before the eye. Given a strong wrist, a rapidly twisting spoon and matron's head pointing in the other direction, it was possible to coax a fair measure of golden goo half-way up the handle.

For their unfailing availability:

> One soon learnt to console the homesick boy or his broken-hearted mother, but weeping fathers (yes, there were some) always defeated me. There was never a dull moment for a prep-school matron.

Always some small boy wanting something – a rubber band, a piece of cloth to make a sail for a boat ('and please could you sew it on for me, matron?') and cotton reels.

For, in some cases, their individuality:

Miss Edwards was short, weather-beaten and as tough as a boot. She always wore the proper starched uniform of a nurse, which was reassuring. She also had a bad squint, which was disturbing, and an open Baby Austin, which carried her off to the delights of Bristol once a week. Another pleasure was her portable gramophone and a huge collection of Frank Crummit recordings which she played incessantly, 'The Gay Caballero', 'Abdul, Abdulbul Amir' and 'Donald the dub (joined a country club)'.

For their medical skills:

Her successor, from 1918 to 1936, is also remembered with affection. She had some strange remedies for nasal complaints; boys with colds were made to sniff at an unnamed liquid over the sink, and her unsuccessful attempt to cure a boy's blocked nostril was to make him try to blow out candles with it every morning. For other ailments the remedy was simple – cascara.

For their failure to be persistently hoodwinked:

. . . Punch and Judy toothpaste, however, soon replaced butter as a popular delicacy. This was discovered to taste every bit as nice as most of the

sweets which constituted the weekly sweet ration.
But there was no limit on toothpaste; it could be
ordered from matron as soon as the last tube was
empty. Gourmets considered banana flavour to be
the best; but unfortunately the rise in toothpaste
consumption was too startling to pass unobserved
and the craze died an early death at matron's
hands . . .

It is hard luck on this devoted band of women that there
should be so little that is cheerful and exciting about the
word 'matron', the name basically meaning, as it does, 'an
elderly lady of staid and sober habits'. Matrons are not seen
to much advantage in literature's pages, with Shakespeare
referring to night as 'thou sober-suited matron, all in
black'. The references to matrons in school hymns are
perilous (giggles) and unfortunate (accusations of im-
pertinence), especially when 'The Son of God goes forth
to war' (Bishop Heber, and No 439) accompanied by,
among others, 'a noble army, men and boys, the matron
and the maid'. One such reference caused trouble for
Siegfried Sassoon when at Marlborough. Required and at
short notice to play the hymn for evening prayers, a
ceremony at which matron was present and to which she
lent her pious alto, he failed to see that the hymn chosen,
No 457, called itself 'For a Holy Matron' and that Verse 2
began with 'Such holy love inflamed her breast'. The
hymn ended there, the furious housemaster yelling 'Let
the music cease!' and hurriedly asking the Almighty to
grant those present knowledge of His truth and in the
world to come life everlasting: and in the interview to
come, a tremendous ticking off.

Never mind. It is, in most cases, recompense enough for
a spinster, as they usually are, to find herself being a

surrogate mother to fifty or so small boys without the pain of having to give them birth and the expense of bringing them up and educating them.

And there are always the pills:

> The matron was rather a frightening figure for some, but a comforting person in real trouble. She would not put up with any nonsense. I can see her now, quite clearly, standing outside the dining-room to pop a quinine pill into our mouths as we emerged. A few brave boys removed the pill as soon as they got past her, and popped it into the open nozzle of the fire hose hanging on the wall further down the passage.

And the stimulating epidemics:

> In those days there were sighs of relief if an Easter Term was survived without a major epidemic; now bad luck is cursed if there is one. When a boy caught an infectious or contagious disease he was, with E.L.B.'s approval, left in contact with the others for a day or two before being sent to the sanatorium; this ensured that a good number also contracted the disease at an age when it was unlikely to be serious, and to save them from catching it, with probably more disturbing effects, at a riper age. Sometimes the policy backfired, as in the Easter Term of 1916 which, in E.L.B.'s words, 'saw a record established as regards infectious illness, perhaps the most virulent epidemic we have ever experienced. We had fifty-two cases of measles, fifty-three of German measles and eight of chicken pox; twenty-six boys had two of these maladies, three had all three, one developed

measles concurrently with German measles and one German measles with chicken pox.'

(Those well versed in the 'New Mathematics' will no doubt wish to draw a Venn Diagram at this point.)

And, finally, we note once more the careful attention to bodily machinery:

One of E.L.B.'s pet themes was the human bodily function. Every term he would declare that, 'The body, laddies, makes a good servant but a very bad master . . .' etc., etc. The school lavatories, being in a separate building, were always euphemistically referred to as 'Across the Way', a term which still exists, even as a noun. In E.L.B.'s time there was a school list on one of the cubicle doors, and every boy had to tick off his name when he had achieved what he had set out for. Those who failed to do so appeared on the nightly defaulters' list, and several dishonourable mentions qualified for the appropriate medical punishment from Mrs Ross, the matron, who was single-minded in her use of Gregory powder. But the scheme was self-defeating, as all ticked off their names, regardless of results, and did the same for friends if they seemed to have forgotten.

9 a.m.

Nine o'clock is the customary time for morning prayers, evening prayers being normally additionally achieved in private and kneeling at the bedside. The nine o'clock variety are conducted by the headmaster and, in cases where the school possesses no chapel, upon a raised platform in some conveniently large assembly point (the gym, the big classroom), with the entire staff grouped in a seemly manner behind him. At one school, this was the moment for examining what colour socks the headmaster had on. They were silk ones, and a red pair indicated an extra half-holiday, while green ones (surely rather a rare colour) meant a whole holiday.

Some headmasters took the subject of religious instruction very seriously and it is reported that one of them 'retired to bed for six weeks at one time in order to revise the Psalms. He would take part of one Psalm and link it with part of another in order to make them more suitable for school use. He really did it rather well and the book was subsequently published as "The Psalter Revised". We always used this version in the school chapel, of course.' Our respect for this innovator is increased on discovering that it was his custom sometimes to say somewhat original prayers. One of them began 'Dear Lord, doubtless Thou

knowest that in the *Daily Telegraph* this morning . . .'
Another headmaster had a rich voice with a trace of a
Yorkshire accent and was unable to pronounce the letter
'r', the boys naturally looking keenly forward to the
Passiontide lesson in Chapel, '. . . and Bawabbas was a
wobber'.

Those who recall the relentless flow of chapel services
will know how welcome was an unusual happening.

> In chapel we were bored, amused and moved in
> turn. There was the deadly repetition in some of
> the services, where I understood hardly a word.
> There was the thrill of the unexpected. One
> evening a cat jumped up on the altar. Enjoyable
> because it represented a threat to the authority to
> which we always had to submit, right or wrong, just

or unjust. How could the master taking the service deal with the situation without looking a fool. We were often made to look foolish by them, how lovely to see the tables turned. He couldn't put the cat into the black book, or tell it to wait outside the study . . . alas, the cat disappeared at the back of the altar and the psalm droned on just as before.

The school called Elmley could always be relied upon for some bizarre happening or other and one day the youthful Lord Berners was 'dared' by a primly religious boy called Creeling to throw his Bible across the room in order to discover in what way the outraged Maker would punish him, Creeling foretelling disasters galore (struck by lightning, bankruptcy, etc). But the only disaster was, as the Bible was describing a graceful arc in the air, the arrival of the headmaster, the appallingly sadistic Mr Gambril. The culprit escaped the birch, the crime being considered too serious for corporal punishment, but was made to stand on a bench and be hissed by the entire school, after which there came a period of social ostracism.

Sanctimonious little boys were always fair game for teasing and the smug Creeling, who 'always looked as if he had just risen from prayer' did not go unmolested. They spread a rumour that he had two sisters called Tabitha and Jane, to whom constant reference was made ('Hullo, Creeling. Written to Tabitha and Jane?'), and he was mercilessly cross-questioned about his God – had He toe-nails and was He ever to be found in the lavatory? And upon Creeling vehemently asserting that He was ubiquitous and was everywhere, there were ceaseless chants of 'Creeling worships a funny sort of God. No toe-nails and lives in the lavatory.'

'I hope that you are a Communicant and that you play

Bridge?' were the final words in a headmaster's letter offering a job to an applicant, and here is an opportunity to examine a few of those who have spent their lives, or part of them, teaching in prep schools. By no means all of them could keep order, and one pillar of the church remembers that, often disturbed by the sounds of chaos coming from the other side of the partition in the big schoolroom, his thoughts strayed irreverently to the hymn words, 'Although thy form we cannot see, We know and feel that thou art there.'

Many schools have had, and rejoiced in, an Oldest Inhabitant who arrived nobody quite remembers when, so long ago is it, and signed on for a probationary term and who has ever since been part of the fixtures and fittings.

> In those days many such replicas of Mr Chips devoted their whole lives to the community that employed them. Partly, no doubt, it was due to economic reasons, for the supply was greater than the demand; but partly also to loyalty and a genuine love of their job. Their long service was a great source of stability and continuity in institutions of this kind.

The longer they stayed, the more painful was the moment of retirement.

> With regard to the other clergyman, Mr Adcock, the only thing one could say about him was that he was very old and very mad. As a teacher he was utterly useless, and I imagine that his services had only been retained for sentimental reasons. He had been a schoolmaster for an incalculable number of years.
>
> I don't know whether Mr Adcock had, in his

early youth, lived on a farm, but he certainly had an agricultural obsession in his old age, and he was for ever using such expressions as 'putting the hand to the plough', 'sowing seeds and reaping', 'calling a spade a spade', and so forth. He used to refer to boys as 'sheep' and 'cows'. When he was annoyed with you he would sometimes call you a 'bad cow'. He was a venerable looking old man with a short straggling white beard and white fluffy hair that used to glow like an aureole when outlined against the light. Indeed he had the air of an elderly saint. Apart from the senile decay from which he was suffering, he was an amiable old man and everybody liked him. He used to praise his pupils ecstatically whenever they did anything right, and he never lost his temper or gave one punishments like the other masters. Towards the end of my time at school he had grown so old and incompetent that he was at last obliged to retire. His farewell sermon was a very moving affair. He got into the pulpit with considerable difficulty, addressed the congregation as 'My good cows,' and then burst into tears.

In some cases, whole staffs are remembered as being in some way strange or unsatisfactory.

At the age of eight I was sent to my preparatory school, Stanmore Park. I was put straight into the top form, only to be demoted after a week to a level more suitable to my age and relative ignorance of everything except Latin grammar. Stanmore Park, I am convinced, was a hell hole. Vernon Royle, the headmaster, was known as 'the Reverend' although not in Holy Orders. He was a famous cricketer. We were told that while he was dozing at cover point one day, a black object hurtled towards him and he caught it. His catch turned out to be a swallow. R. F. Reynolds was a superb shot with a piece of chalk when a boy in his form annoyed him. Nose, cheek, forehead were his preferred targets, in that order; he never hit a boy in the eye. His classroom was on the second floor and he dangled a boy called Openshaw outside the window by his hair. Openshaw was not too popular so we were amused. Another master, D. W. Carr, who was said to have invented the googlie before Bosanquet, got drunk one evening and tried to remove the appendix of a boy called Cremer with a penknife. I was upset when the classics master, J. M. Quinton, who was nice to me, committed suicide in the lavatory of a train.

Here and there, serious misdemeanours have been reported.

At my school, Edward Rée was a beacon of light and hope, with an easy charm and unaffected friendliness. Someone as normal as he was could be regarded as inexpendable there. For the rest of the staff were almost all nondescript or very odd indeed.

Thus there was 'Bully' Beaumont, a fierce old gentleman who bandied no words with children who wouldn't or couldn't learn, but hit them bone-shaking blows in the chest. I felt fairly sick after one of these; it was much worse for Desmond with his weak stomach. Nobody, of course, thought of *complaining*; such an idea would never have occurred to any of us. But the end came for 'Bully' when he aimed one of his haymakers at Andrew Gibbs. A nippy little boxer, Andrew ducked, but took the blow in his eye. A day or two later his father, the Archdeacon of Hatfield, came down to school to see him. As soon as he established that Andrew had *not* been fighting, he went to the head and demanded an inquiry. 'Bully', not a bad man at heart, had to go.

Another master was an epileptic. The masters had their 'Common Room' at the top of a flight of very steep and narrow stairs, and this fellow habitually had his attacks at the top of them. He then fell the whole way down; by some miracle, he never broke his neck.

We would gather round his prostrate body: 'What a swiz!' someone might say. 'He's not even foaming at the mouth today.'

More spectacular was the case of the games master, Mr Fraser (this wasn't his name). He played rugger and cricket well and was quite popular. Then one day I wrote this letter home:

'Dear Mummy and Daddy, I hope you are well. A strange thing happened on Wednesday. Mr Fraser was bowling to us in the nets when a big black car drove up behind the cricket pavilion. Three men got out of it, and two of them, wearing mackintoshes, came across to the nets. Mr Fraser saw them closing in and made a run for it (he used to play for the Harlequins). But one tackled him low, the third man came running, and the three men put him in the black car and drove away. We haven't seen him since.'

My mother was scandalized and wrote a letter to the head, asking him how a sports master could be kidnapped in broad daylight and whether the police had been informed.

The head answered that it was the police who had taken Mr Fraser away. He was very angry with them himself, as they had driven into the school grounds without his permission. Mr Fraser had been passing dud cheques in various places and was now 'helping the police with their enquiries'.

Mr Fraser was replaced by Mr Westerburn (also not his real name). He was not popular at all; for one thing, he seemed to be no good at all at cricket and he had a shifty manner. Then one day he, too, disappeared, but this time there was an explanation – the head told the school that he had taken 'employment of a different kind'. In a sense this was true. For Mr Westerburn, too, had been passing dud cheques and was being detained at His Majesty's pleasure.

Many tributes have come in to dedicated and obviously talented teachers, even those who had to struggle away to inspire enthusiasm in that, to some, least arousing scholastic subject, Latin.

Despite all this, we all owe the 'old man' an incalculable debt for introducing us to one of the finest Latin masters in the country. He joined the staff in 1938, a pot-bellied, middle-aged, balding bachelor who smelt strongly of beer after lunch. He was a brilliant teacher of Latin and was well known for the number of scholarships he had obtained at top public schools. His methods may now appear somewhat crude, for although they were staggeringly successful in implanting an indelible knowledge of Latin grammar, they achieved no success at all in teaching Latin as a history or a literature or a culture. He was concerned solely with North and Hillard and Kennedy's *Revised Latin Primer*, the contents of which books he rammed into us by the sternest discipline and with unremitting and brainwashing repetition. He was eccentric, shy, quasi-academic and a figure of fun. But we all genuinely loved him. When he died, I had my own tribute to his goodness published in the *Times*, which gave tremendous personal satisfaction. I felt it was a kind of atonement for the merciless way I had ragged him.

This unique, pipe-smoking, deep-voiced, Pickwickian character had nevertheless the dice heavily loaded on his side, for we had more periods a week devoted to Latin than to any other subject. In addition he insisted on extra coaching after lunch for the scholarship candidates; he absolutely lived and breathed Latin, and if you happened to be able to take it in such large doses you were bound to do well, for you were two or three years ahead of your time at the end of it all. (The economics of education were never seriously regarded.)

He made us learn Kennedy's grammar by heart. Particularly the rules of syntax at the back, the prepositional phrases and the gender rhymes. We learned definitions, examples and exceptions till we could say them in our sleep. They had no reference outside the pages of the grammar, however, and I can recall no conscious attempt to interpret them in any kind of living context. They were learned like the parts of a play; sentences, titles, quotations and tags with no apparent relevance at all. One picked up English grammar this way, of course, but that was merely a by-product. The ablative absolute, for example, was learned as a construction whose value lay in how to do it rather than the thing done. Maybe he had a point!

We learned the gender rhymes as a piece of end-of-term light relief. They were never of much use because the words involved were mostly too rare to be encountered in even the most advanced 'unseen' or prose exercise unless one happend to have to translate such sentences as 'The dropsy-stricken husband met the fornicator by the Adriatic sea.' Yet as a kind of doggerel the gender rhymes had an irresistible appeal. They had a speed and a rhythm that were captivating, a warmth and humour lacking in any other aspect of learning Latin.

Back again to the oddities.

There was hardly one of the masters at my first school who wasn't slightly crazy in one way or another. The art master, for example, an ex-army sergeant with a fine waxed moustache, affected an exaggerated Oxbridge accent, except that he emphatically and unfailingly missed off every aitch where it should have been and put one on where it shouldn't. In consequence he was mimicked, with varying degrees of success, by every boy in the school. But for the genuinely asinine, Tubby was the man. There was an occasion in a Junior House match, which Tubby was umpiring, when a boy was given out by him and neither the boy, nor anyone else, knew the reason. Asked by the scorer at the end of the innings, Tubby at first could not remember, but then it came back to him 'Oh yes,' he said, 'it was for waving his bat about in a ridiculous manner.' The same Tubby was once unwise enough to explain his system of marking essays – yes, he taught English – to the class. 'Now the first essay was really quite good so I gave the boy nine marks out of ten, but then I came to Johnson's, which was at least two marks better, so I had to give him eleven out of ten' . . . and so on. You can imagine that, after this, he was as clay in the hands of the quick-witted pupil and one boy told me that he had managed to score fifteen out of ten.

And yet again.

The school got its fair share of public school scholarships, so I suppose the teaching of the other masters was sound, but I cannot believe that a stranger set of instructors were ever got together. Rawlings, who taught the first form, used habitually to read the *Sporting Times* in school with his feet up on the desk until the time came for him to hear us construe. Daubeny, the master of the second form, had no thought but for the encouragement of a small moustache; Davy of the third form used mostly to be asleep; Geoghehan of the fourth (called 'Geege') had lost his right arm, and used always to have some favourite in his class, who sat on his knee in school time and was an important personage, for he could, if you were friends with him, always persuade Geege not to report misconduct to Waterfield. One such boy, now a steady

hereditary legislator, I well remember; he pulled Geege's beard, and altered the marks in his register, and ruled him with a rod of iron. Geege was otherwise an effective disciplinarian, and had an unpleasant habit, if he thought you were not attending, of spearing the back of your hand with the nib of his pen, dipped in purple ink. Then there was a handwriting specialist called Prior who gave out stationery on Saturdays. His appearance was always hailed by a sort of Gregorian chant to which the words were, 'All boys wanting ink go to Mr Prior.' Then came Mr Voltaire, the gay young Frenchman, and these, with one or two more of whom I cherish no recollection, all lived together at a house in East Sheen called Clarence House and were, I think, a shade more frightened of Waterfield than we.

Three more unusual characters deserve to be remembered.

These prayers were probably graced by the presence of the school chaplain, The Reverend Septimus Philpott (otherwise known as 'Old Seppy'), brother of the headmaster and a somewhat eccentric character who used to proceed from his home to the school in a flowing surplice and with his hands stretched out in front of him. He was reputed to be intensely conscious of the possibility of suffering harm from any germs with which he came in contact and accordingly, when he reached a gate or other obstacle, he would wait until he could summon a boy to open it for him.

Inevitably, during war-time with the increasingly chronic shortage of teachers, there were difficulties of personality. One distinctly unusual parson, engaged for the start of a Michaelmas term, arrived half-way through the following February in a blinding snowstorm, preached quite a good sermon, and the next day vanished for ever. Another, still living in the past, was chiefly remembered for removing his jacket and waistcoat and sighing nervously before venturing to use the telephone.

Quaint and pleasing incidents abound in the recollections of those far-off years.

There was, for instance, the Great Rice Pudding Strike and a melodramatic occasion when the music master (later a cathedral organist) had chastized a boy, strictly against the 'Rules', in a fit of temper. The whole school conspired to be silent throughout a meal; in its way the perfect protest. One old boy recalls how, in the course of it, he was erroneously accused as a ringleader and publicly expelled. Afterwards he was pardoned on production of a watertight alibi; at the crucial time he had been playing chess with the German master.

There were those merry catch-phrases in which schoolboys delight, every utterance increasing their appeal, one of which was a sentence in an unfortunate lecture by a pioneer bird-photographer: ''Ere we 'ave the Common Tern a-sittin' on 'er nest.' There were schoolmasterly jokes, as for instance when some boys who had damaged the chain and bucket of a well on a neighbouring farm were told to write out five hundred times 'Let well alone.' There was one master's jovial way of dismissing the school, table by table, after a meal: 'Go, bunk, vamoose, hook it, skedaddle' and so forth ('This was looked on as the highest form of humour.'). There was the reply to a mother who telephoned to ask if her son was homesick ('I very much hope that he is. I shouldn't think much of his home if he wasn't.'). There was the headmaster who, giving out rail tickets at the end of term, was heard to say to a boy who was loudly protesting that he lived in Sussex, 'Laddie, if ye have a ticket to Inverness, ye go to Inverness.' There was the staff's pleasure in a schoolboy's essay on The Holidays ('We are all met at Victoria by our expectant mothers.'). There was the happy moment when a parent, left alone in the headmaster's study, picked up a book with a very classical-sounding title on the dust-cover but found that it contained a copy of *Racing Up to Date*.

It is agreeable to discover that, by and large, school-masters and their teaching are remembered with gratitude.

Every prep school must have *one* master who can be relied on to stay with the school for more than one year, who can pass on to the boys his inspirations, his *joie de vivre*, and B. Cummins was just that; we had time to get to know him, he passed on his enthusiasm for literature effortlessly and captured our imagination. He was rather lazy and for much of the time he let us get on with our work while he manicured his nails, fingers and toes, and polished his superb sandals. When *he* was self-engrossed, *we* were self-engrossed. He had presence, so our behaviour in class matched his. He often ended his lessons with a Saki story which he read quietly and drily. Often at four o'clock he would rush away in his little car to the BBC at Bristol to read on *Children's Hour* 'The Adventure of Hep-zibah the Hen'. He was about thirty and unmarried, but in the 1940's he met a Russian princess, married her and vanished. He it was who, quite effortlessly, put on our dramatic productions, including a performance of *Lady Precious Stream* for the Chinese. His reading of *Shridni Vashtar* will haunt me for ever.

And how pleasant that classroom jokes remain the same down the years.

The master of the second form, Mr Grey, was a humorist. He was always making little jokes and his classroom perpetually rang with merry laughter. His jokes were not always quite on the same level, and at times the laughter was perhaps a little perfunctory. Some of them had the persistence of a recurring decimal. There was a line in Horace, '*celeri saucius malus africano*'. Whenever it occurred Mr Grey would give a wink and say, 'Now, boys, don't translate that by "Celery sauce is bad for the African".' But he strongly discouraged his pupils from attempting to make jokes in their turn. If you ever tried to be funny yourself, he would look at you severely and say, 'You're a bit of a wag, aren't you?'

10 a.m.

Work is in progress and pens are scratching away (at my prep school, you began with pencils and were only promoted to ink when you were considered sufficiently mature – about eleven or so – not to spill it and make messes). Adult voices drone on, the droning having a specially soporific effect on warm summer days. Now and again, a loud burst of happy laughter indicates that a joke has been made, or it may be that a master who cannot yet keep order (a skill that has, like any other, to be learnt) has yet again been made a fool of.

Until quite recently, the generally dreaded classics were considered to be a vital part of the school curriculum.

> Latin stood unchallenged at the centre of the curriculum, and grammar was the key to Latin. The working day began with a lesson before breakfast, and prep finished at eight in the evening. The dreaded Saturday Evening Paper did not feature football and racing results, but was a test on the week's work: those who performed inadequately were denied the Saturday evening entertainment, and did extra work instead. There were other, more conventional punishments as well.

And not only Latin.

> Another occasion that sticks out in my mind is the time we were doing a GGP (would you believe it, a Greek Grammar Paper!) and Billy said that he would beat anyone who wrote a particular genitive singular incorrectly. I did and I was on the spot. So enthusiastic was Billy about the classics and literature in general that every year plays were performed which would include the whole school. The youngest would do a comparatively simple play and there would be a short English play by the next youngest. The French master produced a comedy in French, the English master one from Shakespeare and Billy would do one in Latin and one in Greek. Billy, I suspect, had much the same effect on our parents as he had on us, because they all laughed dutifully and clapped rather over-loudly, although I am sure that the sight of Xerxes whipping the sea was so much Greek to them!

Schoolmasters' admiration of Latin has always been fairly widespread.

> He regarded Latin as the most important subject. Sometimes if boys were weak in Latin, he would stop their work in other subjects in order that they should catch up. He expected the boys to move on to Virgil and Livy, which he taught, surprisingly, with translations. If used 'scientifically', he said, the translations could help the boys to learn very fast, and indeed he noted that Brown was tackling difficult authors 'in a most dashing manner'.

For one thing, an exam in Latin was then essential for entry to Oxbridge and even though nowadays the classics would appear to be fighting a rear-guard action (one headmaster has been known to refer to his classical VI form as 'a small flag flying very high', a remark that smacks of both defiance and failure), there are still those who would defend the so-called 'disciplines' involved.

It is much to be regretted that Latin appears to be on the way out. There will, of course, be many schoolboys whose peaked caps will reach to the skies in jubilation at this release from academic tyranny; yet many others will doubtless feel a stab of sorrow that such a hallowed, firmly entrenched discipline seems at last to have been discredited. It's as if all those spiritless opponents of the classical classroom had been proved right in the end; I can hear the savage mocking of my erstwhile colleagues whose memory now is but a list of names in alphabetical order.

For the study of Latin was almost the *modus vivendi* of my prep school. Conventionally (and perhaps rather pointlessly) named after a saint, the school would more appropriately have been called Livy or Ovid, for I do not recall, in all the seven years I was there, being told one single fact about the saint whose name we worked and played under; his life had apparently lost all significance. 'Green Cedars' would have done, or even 'The Hilltop Educational Establishment for the sons of well-to-do Industrial Managers'. For such were my compatriots. The responsibility for this policy of unflagging commitment to Latin must, of course, be laid at the door of the headmaster. I can only suppose it was the result of a narrowness of

approach that would nowadays mark him down as
wholly unfit to have charge of youth. Indeed one
suspects that his 'policy' for running the school
was no more than a repetition of his own experience
some fifty years earlier.

In addition to the daily Latin lesson, other subjects were
studied.

> Empire was much emphasized. We coloured it all
> on maps we had drawn on Mercator's Projection
> with no warning about the distortions produced by
> that device. Our best mapping, however, was of the
> Middle East for, in the name of scripture, we were
> required to chart the maraudings of Joshua and the
> cruises and hikes of St Paul. The master demanding
> all this seemed unaware of any theological paradox
> in the two accounts of, presumably, the same deity.
> It did occur to a few of us boys, but the inquiring
> mind was not encouraged and we asked no questions.
> In English, French and Latin it may well have been
> a necessary chore to dwell on the mechanics of
> grammar without any hint of linguistic joys in store,
> apart from whatever stimulus we drew from Joshua,
> the Acts and the Pied Piper of Hamelin. Neither
> 'sur le pont d'Avignon' nor Caesar's tedious *de
> bello Gallico* inspired me at all, but I suppose our
> mentors had to score the material goals, the Com-
> mon Entrance passes. Mathematics were taught
> very heavily, science not at all and history without
> colour, save for that on our maps.

But at one school there was an unusual innovation.

Despite some resistance he managed to get a few

regular science periods on to the timetable in the
1920s, and he gave the boys an introduction to
general science at a time when it was taught in very
few prep schools. A great relief from the very
formally taught main curriculum subjects, science
was not universally approved of, partly because it
was not yet considered 'respectable', and partly
because it was so popular with the boys. In the
well-equipped science room they were taught that
the atom was the ultimate in indivisibility and that
splitting it would bring about the end of the world.
'Home-made' experiments were a delight; in the
science classes run by Fewings, and later J. D.
Harrison as well, cans were filled with gases and
blasted up to the ceiling amid cheers. Such was
the attraction of the subject and the conjurer in
charge of it that the room was full of activity in the
evenings after tea. The boys weighed things, boiled
things, gave themselves supervized electric shocks
and watched experiments, to the accompaniment
of '78' records on the old 'His Master's Voice' type
of gramophone.

At another school, and as long ago as the 1920s, 'the boys
learnt, and apparently enjoyed, shorthand. They worked
at it by themselves in play hours, by writing notes to one
another and witticisms on the blackboards.' And there were
other pleasures:

There was also a dancing class in the autumn term,
but no small girls. I did, however, on one occasion
enjoy female society – entrancing creatures in blue
dresses and bright green hair-ribbons. With another
small boy I was lent to a local girls' school for a

Red Cross practical examination. The girls found our pressure points, applied tourniquets, bandaged us all over and gave us artificial respiration. We found it all delightful and were rewarded with a large box of chocolates.

It is pleasant to discover the extent to which reading was encouraged. Here we are back in the early 1900s.

Literature was not absolutely tabooed. There was a school library from which we could borrow books every Sunday. The two most popular authors of the day were Henty and Jules Verne. They were respectively the Apostles of Manliness and Imagination. Boys could practically be divided into two categories, those who liked Henty and those who preferred Jules Verne. Henty had the larger following. I sampled a few of his works, but I soon found out that there was a disappointing monotony in his literary invention. The stories were, all of them, very much alike, there was for ever the same boy-hero, merely transposed to different historical and geographical backgrounds, in an atmosphere overcharged with a rather mawkish patriotism.

Jules Verne, on the other hand, led one into a new universe of marvels. His books comprised every subject that one could possibly dream of. His readers were introduced to every quarter of the globe, were invited to explore every possibility of the future. In those days, on the eve of the appearance of motor-cars, submarines and aeroplanes, his novels had a prophetic glamour. In one of them, *The Castle of the Carpathians*, there was even a foretaste of the Talkies. Such books as these, one felt, might have been approved of for their mere educational value. Geography could be learnt more graphically and more agreeably in a story like *Round the World in Eighty Days* than in any primer of the school curriculum. Yet Jules Verne was not wholly approved of by the school authorities. I suppose it was feared that his influence might lead to dangerous excesses of the imagination.

Fashions in schoolboy reading change and by the end of the First World War school libraries were having to stock a much more vigorous type of 'yarn', as the popular word was.

The reading habits of the boys were significantly changed by the war. Westerman and Henty went out of fashion. Nobody was interested in *The Sea-Girt Fortress* or *The Lion of St Mark's*; nobody wanted to go *With Roberts to Kandahar*, nor yet *With Kitchener to Khartoum*. A new breed of author took over the market with such titles as *The Secret Service Submarine* and *The Secret Service Airoplane* (contemporary spelling). Commander Lawless R.N. and Buckle of Submarine V2 fought gallantly for King and Country. Heroes, most of whom seemed to be named Frank, uttered such deathless lines as, 'Come on, you cowardly bunch of cads: one British seaman is worth the whole blithering pack of you.' While, for some reason best known to E.L.B., detective novels of any sort were banned absolutely, titles such as *Count Dracula*, *Ultus, the Man from the Dead* and *The Clutching Hand* were approved dormitory reading. But the basic literary diet consisted of the colossal annuals *Chums* and the *Boys' Own Paper*. Once in the school, one of these volumes became public property and was avidly read by anyone who picked it up. The *BOP* was full of useful information, while *Chums* largely contained armchair soldiers' interpretations of events on the Western Front. Anti-German schoolboy literature was a not unnatural product of the First World War. It still flourishes.

Children in general are fond of being read aloud to and Maurice Baring speaks warmly of evenings when the headmaster, an otherwise fairly chilly man, read them *Treasure Island* and *The Moonstone* and passages from *Pickwick*. It makes for agreeable and cosy evenings and of course we find the same thing going on at that enlightened school, St Andrew's.

Every Sunday evening the boys would go into the sitting room to listen to a story. In a great semicircle at E.L.B.'s feet before a roaring fire they heard him read such books as *Three Men in a Boat*, *Moonfleet* and *King Solomon's Mines*, in instalments. His own favourite was *The Moonstone*, which he read for the first time in 1892 and for the last time in 1932. Boiled sweets were handed round. Boys who preferred not to listen to the readings could look at magazines, or view the splendours of Nippon and Cathay on a stereoscope. The livelier element could go to the dining-room and play war games with lead soldiers. Three of E.L.B.'s brothers were with him on the staff, and it was not uncommon during the Sunday evening story for one of them, Mr Charlie, to creep through the drawing room in the direction of the cellar and return a few moments later with a glass of port, which he took away to drink in peace.

11 a.m.

Morning break and, with the staff busy recovering from their teaching exertions, swapping howlers and irritations while ingesting doughnuts and mugs of strong Indian tea in their common room, the first proper chance for the school bullies to get going. At Stirling Court it was the accepted thing to be bullied until you were about eleven and a half years old. A favourite ploy was for an older boy to approach you and enquire whether you knew the two kinds of champagne. 'No' you answered fearfully, though by then knowing them only too well – but the answer 'Yes' might have secured you a kick as well. He would then seize one's side-burns, such as they were, and pulling down on them, which wasn't too bad, announce 'That's sham pain.' The reverse and pulling up process then took place and was agony, one's shrieks being greeted with 'That's real pain!' 'Oh I see,' one said, between sobs.

But at eleven and a half or so, it was, so to speak, your turn and cravenly one followed the herd and lashed away at any cowering figure who was currently being bullied. I recall with deepest shame a boy called Lenville being permanently in tears (it was quite fatal to blub, for it only drove bullies to further excesses) and trying to enlist my support. Photographs reveal my face at the time as resembling a large and innocent balloon and Lenville evidently and foolishly thought that I must be good at heart. His mother came down one summer weekend and, at her son's request, took me out with him for an extremely lavish tea at a local tea-garden called 'Hove-To', the district being full of retired naval persons. Friendliness reigned but when she had gone, Lenville was of course immediately set upon and prominent among the whackers was myself. At one point he turned round and directed a tear-drenched look at me. '*You*!' he said. 'And my mother took you out to tea and gave you strawberries!' Appalling guilt is with me yet, grows worse year by year, and will haunt me until the grave.

New boys usually got, naturally, the worst of it.

Somebody is whimpering in the rhododendrons. I am unhappy already but this makes me feel frightened as well. 'You're just a filthy little new kid,' I can hear someone saying. That's P. A. Stamford's voice. He is the worst bully in the school. 'Boot him again, Hollis,' Stamford says. I can hear the sound of Hollis booting. He plays right back for the second eleven and is a very good kick. 'That's what you get for being a new kid, see?' says Stamford.

I am a new kid too, I keep thinking. P. A. Stamford hates all new kids – in fact he hates nearly everybody except those who are nearly as good at bullying as he is. He doesn't touch Dorrien-Smith though. Dorrien-Smith is very fierce but he isn't a bully. He sometimes punches one in the wind when passing, but this is just because he is a natural fighter. He doesn't do it to be unkind. Dorrien-Smith comes from the Scilly Isles which is possibly what makes him so fierce and tough.

This school is hidden in pine trees and rhodo-dendrons. I wonder how many tears have been shed in those rhododendrons. Buckets and buckets I should think. I swear I'll never plant rhododendrons when I grow up.

Next Sunday is 'Blub Sunday'. 'Blub Sunday' is the day when everybody pays off old scores. At least that's the idea, but actually it is just an excuse for the bullies to get at anybody. I am told that I am certain to be made to blub on Sunday. Peacock and I have made a pact to stick very close together and come to the defence of the other one if he is attacked first. I hope I have the guts to stick up for Peacock if he is attacked and not me. I wonder who had the brainy wheeze to invent 'Blub Sunday'. P. A. Stamford, I suppose.

Schofield has run away! Apparently Schofield's mother had been to see Foxy and told him why. Apparently it was just because he was being bullied by Hollis and P. A. Stamford and he just couldn't stand it any more. It wouldn't be much good me running away because my parents are abroad.

The whole school is buzzing with excitement. Foxy is going to talk to the whole school at eleven o'clock. I wonder what it is all about.

This is the best day of my whole life! P. A. Stamford has been demonitorized! Foxy said it had come to his ears that there had been some bad cases of bullying lately and that he wasn't going to have it in his school. He said that it had also come to his ears that the principal offender was P. A. Stamford and that, in order to make a public example of him, he was to be demonitorized. Stamford was sitting there just next to Foxy. He looked just the same as usual, only a little paler. This is a tremendous weight off my mind. What about Hollis though?

Every night I am hungry. After I have said my prayers I lie awake for hours thinking of the sausages we have on Sundays. I wonder when this misery will all end. One can only bear it because there's nothing – absolutely nothing – else one can do.

Bullies usually liked to vary their methods of persecution and frequently devised quite sophisticated tortures.

Longworth minor had the reputation of being a bully. He was in the third form and was a member (if not the actual ringleader) of a very objectionable band of youths in the same form, whose object in life seemed to be to torment and harass the smaller boys whenever they got the chance. They had constituted themselves into a sort of *Vehmgericht*, a Council of Ten, and the most sinister rumours of their terroristic methods were being circulated.

The third form classroom was at the far end of one of the wings and was reached by a flight of stairs leading to that classroom only. Opening out of it was a smaller room that was never used, partly because it was rather dark and partly because there was no other access to it except through the third form classroom itself. This room had been organized by Longworth minor and his friends as a torture-chamber for the punishment of anyone who happened to incur their displeasure.

Those who had suffered in the torture-chamber gave the most hair-raising accounts of it. One marvelled at their ever having managed to survive. The tortures were various and refined. One of them consisted in placing the victim's wrists in two jagged, semicircular holes cut in the top edge of a locker and then pressing down the lid. Another consisted in tying the victim's hands behind his back and pulling them upwards by means of a rope slung over a beam, a form of torture much favoured by the Spanish Inquisition and in mediaeval Germany. In the art of inflicting physical agony even Mr Gambril might have learnt a thing or two.

The dark exploits of the band spread terror among the smaller boys. The staircase leading to the third form classroom, up which, one felt, victims might at any moment be dragged to their doom, acquired all the grim associations of the Bridge of Sighs.

Constant dormitory supervision was an impossibility and the lack of it provided bullies with valuable opportunities.

There was a character called Spedder whose capacity for organized crime was of a high order in one so young. It was Spedder who dreamed up and practised a number of excesses that accounted for my first feelings of real fear. And, like all bullies, he would sometimes be so charming that one ingenuously thought he had seen the light of reason. Spedder inspired a lame following; his henchmen were powerless on their own, yet electrified by his leadership. One of Spedder's little tricks was 'running the gauntlet', when, merely to suit his whimsy, you would suddenly be compelled to strip to the waist and run round the washbasins in the

middle of the dormitory while all the others stood
by their beds and lashed out at you with knotted
ties as you went past. A more barbaric method of
gratifying Spedder's ego was to submit to his
invention of 'stool treatment', in which you lay on
the floor on your back with your legs hooked up
underneath a piano stool on which Spedder sat
whipping your bottom with his own patented
thong.

For the bullied there was little chance of escape. Sometimes
an observant master or headmaster's wife might suspect
that all was not well, but to put on a woebegone face was
considered to be a form of sneaking and not even the badly
bullied sneaked. There was, in sad fact, literally nobody to
whom you could have gone with your troubles, and least
of all could you pour them out in letters home.

Sunday noon

On Sundays in most prep schools, once the required religious observance was safely over (either in their own chapel or in the local church) a noonday hush settled on the building, broken by the scratching of pens and, every so often, the deep sighs customary in those who are reluctantly composing prose. Schoolboys do not cheerfully write letters, even to loved ones, but the Sunday letter could not be escaped and its accomplishment was as formal as a lesson in class. The letters had usually to be left open in order that the master on duty could read them through and make sure that they contained no damagingly accurate facts. There are, very rightly, no instances reported of attempts to improve the letters' literary style or content, or to correct their spelling. They were despatched on Sunday afternoons in those days when the Post Office lived to serve its public and there was a daily post out (and I can even remember, at Stirling Court, a Sunday post in, for it was then that my mother's weekly letter, carefully timed to cheer my Sunday, arrived). It never crossed anybody's mind, such was our fully justified postal faith, that the letter would not reach next day the parental breakfast table, however far away that table might be.

There follows a selection of letters whose spelling

mistakes should in no way be blamed on the printer. They are in no particular order or group, for who can group the ungroupable?

My dearest Mummy,

I've got some quite exciting news this week. The fourth game played rugger this week. Oetzmann got a scholarship at Radley. Exciting item number three; 1st XV beat Ascham St Vincents 13–0 Tuesday, 2nd XV beat ditto 3–0 ditto. That's all the rugger. Hockey; 1st XI lost to Hill Brow 3–4, 2nd XI beat ditto 5–0.

Enter tonight is a puppy show, sorry Puppet. There was a very good film on Sunday called 'The curfew shall not ring tonight', followed by an 'Aesop's Fable', followed by a comedy film featuring Harold Lloyd called 'I couldn't tell you', at least that's what Mr Giddins said it was. Please try not to send my papers so late, as they will run into next week's. I have been having some throwing practice with Mr Carter, and some catching with Liddell (and a hard ball). That of course is ready for next term. Mr Charlie says that the headmaster won't get better in this world, but he'll get better in the next. Dr Sherwood has almost given him up, and he has a Red Cross nurse and two other nurses. Some people say it's a matter of hours, others say days and some say weeks. But I think that there is no hope at all, and I expect you agree. It is, of course, old age, and I think we've seen him for the last time. Yes, we certainly have, for he is dead. No, I'm not joking or anything like that. He is dead, isn't it sad? He died last night, while we were having an extremely good enter. You know, the puppet show. It was awfully well done. But now I want to change the subject about the headmaster, for it is not very pleasant. I can't find another pen anywhere, I know I've got one, but we're not allowed to wander about, but as I'm going to stop. Latin, 2, Maths, 3, and French, as usual, 1.

Heaps of love from
David

Dear Mum,

How are you? I am fine. Thank you very much for your letter. I am writing this letter on the bord thing I got in my stocking so it should be neater. But I dought it is much neater. Right now on to things at school. On Monday it was a pretty boaring day except for games because we had the

master who took the firsts game and he wanted to
see us because he needed three people for the 2nd
team and he said (on monday) that I might go into
the first game but I didn't so I have a good chance
to get into the third team. On Tuesday I went to a
party. After that I had woodwork and I started to
make a pencil box. On Wednesday I had table-
tennis and I played against Oliver and so natraly it
was great fun. After that I had chess and I beat
someone in chess and lost to him in draughts. On
thursday I had cricket choaching and I did quite
well. On Saturday I went out with Gavin and he
has got a dog called Rags. Today the film is Super-
man. How is evryone. I'll phone soon. The trousers
arrived in very good time. And we don't have a
fourth team. See you nexted weekend.

love from Harry

Dear Mummy and Daddy,

      Nothing good about this school. On Tuesday
Action Man went for a walk and hambushed the
boys.

love from Pippin

Dear Mummy and Daddy,

      I hope you are well. I am NOT . . . I have
got a tempricher I am in srgry in big Egipt. The
last time I had my tempricher taken it was 99; the
time bifor it was 101. I went in on Friday the day
we were going to have a jusey test. sorry there isn'int
much news be-koss I've bene in surrgry. I hope you
are well again.

love from Hugh

P.S. Give my love to Pippha

Thank you for your letter. On Saturday we played Ludgrove the score was 12–0. we won cloloures were awarded to Chalmess, tait, Batt F and Spikernell. The matches were good. I am doing a proget on ships my orders were F 12, M 10, E 14. I did quit well in Maths I got no stars this week and 3 conduck marks. I hope you are well. I am too.

love from Hugh

There has been a lot of rain. yesterday 1st XI drawed, the same with under 11 and we lost in the 2nd XI. Next Saturday it is Sports. all three matchs were agentst Lambrook and on Wedsday we lost agenst Ludgrove. I am gowing to Longleat were ther are loins and tigers as my expeditions. I hope you are well I am well tomorrow there is Common entrance. I hope Pipper is well with the dogs and gin-eypigs.

love from Hugh

. . . tomorrow it is the governors meeting and House Half. there are swimming tests today but I did'ent want to go into any so I did not sing on any of the lists. In the paters match they won by 1 wicket.

Darling Mummy and Daddy,

Thank you very much for the letter it was lovely. We have started our EXAM they are lovely the others might not like them but I do, they are quite fun, the only exam I hate was FRENCH it was awful because Mr Webster had not done the Arithmatic exam for us so that we had to have an hour so I hated; All the other exams were lovely.

Thank you very much for the CHRISTMAS stamps they are lovely I am sending one of them on this letter. We had the Christmas pudding it was lovely and we had sixpinces in them. A boy called Bulman had some coconuts sent him and we all had a bit.

love Antony x x x x

My dear all,

Thank you for the letter from Dad and Waddles. I am extremely pleased you are coming home to England.

We had a pleasant visit by the Zeps I was awake and heard it firing and then we heard a crash and then another and the dore opened and Mr Nicles came in. Then he said 'downstairs down to the drawing-room quickly'. But before that Jimmy Hall woke up the dormitory captain (Serra) and said 'Something wrong! Something wrong!' Dead silence no explotions, 'there isn't,' said Serra and went to sleep again. About three seconds after he had gone off again then more explosions 'there's some wrong' said Jimmy, dormatry captain wakes up; dead silience no explotions and bombs dropped; 'there is something around wake up' said Jimmy. The dore opened and Mr Nicles entered.

Hugh Malison refused to get out of bed till he knew what had hapened. James Hall thought the end of the world had come becouse he had been reading a paper about the end of the world. we saw a few holes made by the bombs.

with lots of love to all from Tony.

. . . Yesterday in the evening we had the Debating Society, it was the best one of the term. After McDowall had read the minuits of the last Debate, Sutton went up to a box and picked out two debates. The first was that Sago was preferred to Chewing Gum and the second was that Laberinth was better than Squash. The first debate was most marvellous fun and I will try to tell you what I said. First of all I am sure that it would not look very appertising if you found half a slice of chewing gum on your plate. And then I said, another word for Sago and school is frog eyes and anyway Sago at this school is hardly liked by anyone and I hate it. So I said I would perhaps prefer chewing gum. Chewing gum won 7–4. The 2nd was Laberinth to Squash. Laberinth is a board with lots of holes in and you have got to get past them you start and 1 and end up at 60. The house was defeated and Squash won 8–2. I spoke in this debate as well but I needn't tell you what I said, but I voted Squash. Then Minster went up to the Box and picked one out and it was whether the Piltdown man was preferred to the ape. The house was again defeated 6–4. Nobody said much in this and I didn't but if Mummy doesn't know you better tell her. Then Fox went up and picked one out. It was whether the wireless was preferred to Telivision. The house won 6–5 after a very close debate, I again spoke in this one. And was contridicted by McDowall. On Monday we played Sunningdale it was a draw 0–0.

Dear Mummy and Daddy,

Thank you very much for the letter you sent me. I got the little cases for the Jubilee crowns.

Matron has given me my new cricket boots. They are very nice and they fit me nicely. I have been in bed for nearly five days with a temperature. By my window in the hospital a bird made a nest and laid its eggs there and then the eggs hatched and now there are some beautiful chicks. Yesterday I was allowed to get up because I was much better. Two of our masters (Mr Barcly-Jones and Mr Beazley) have joined the Ladycross choir and sing with the choir. The choir is better now because they joined.

I heard that France won the Eurovision Song Contest, Britain came second and Eire third. Were the songs good?

During Mass today while we were having Holy Communion Fathers trousers fell down. He tried to pull them up but he couldn't so he took them off. I am longing to see you on Saturday.

love from Michael   x x x

Dearest Mummy,

I want a STYLO very much. I love those animals. Will you buy me another 9d set of stamps which Battle gave me for Christmas. Tell Flory I cannot write to her this week, as it will be time very soon. We went to church this morning. I am rather homesick as I cried a great amount this morning.

Will you give the enclosed letter to Nanny. This is the list of things I want for my birthday

Stamp Catalogue 'Stylow' Talking doll or a walking sailor.   Type Writer.

Will you give this PC to Flory with my love.

Miss James was very pleased with the cards.

Just as I came in we had a game of Bridge. Will you send my paintbox and a painting book to amuse me because I am rather unhappy. I hope this letter will not worry you. But I like telling you all my troubles. Will you please send those mackintoshes toffie advertisements every week, and I will pay you for the postage.

Ebsworth insists on writing to thank you, but I say he need not. I gave the other frog to Maxwell who loved it. I am dreading to-morrow because of Latin Ex. I am certain to get a licking.

You do not mind me telling you all my troubles. Oh dear there are such a lot of days to come and so many weeks. Now I must end up my letter.

with

love

from

peter

Darling Mummy and Daddy

Thank you very much for the parchsul and the cake it is lovily. I am going to be very careful with your pen. We had it, you now what I mean the cack, on Friday day that is the day it came. Do you think that I can have you coming to see me on some day that you can manch. If Aunt prakin can wants to now why I have not ritten to her is because I cannot find a nice time to rite to her. I will tell you why not find a nice time to right to her because we have got to have football or horkey. I mostley play football. But yesterday played horkey it is lovly. I am longing to see you again. You h. . . .

Sunday   You have nit come to see me for

agses and I am longing to see you again. So you must come and see me. We had lovly Game of football yesterday. It is so good that only four more Sundays till I come home. We are going to have a play about Robin Hood. I am on Ex 48 and. I have got a orful big brouse where Brock shiner. One of the boys made some snow shoes. We had I must go now.

> ps In the play I am going to be a woman.
>> lots of love   Ant.

Dear Mother,

> Mr Hawtrey is very pleased at my progress. This is the List.

1 White Maj	10 Scott	20 Tandy
2 Rodgerson	11 Watney	21 Looker
3 Berresford	12 Gregory	22 Isacce
4 White min	13 Weyman	23 BULL
5 Ebsworth	14 Ouvry	24 Horn
6 Riddle	15 Shappe	25 Burnett
7 Greaham	16 Clarke	26 Jameson
8 Maxwell	17 Goodbody	
9 Jhonson	18 Oak Rhind	
	19 Cooper	

with love from Peter

Dear Mummie,

> I have only got one envlope. I am sending you a little or rather a big booklet of dr benadows homes. I am writing with an OTHER founten pen. do look out for childrens our becouse the man is going to lecher about the same thing. do come and see me and tell me when you are coming nex.

I scord my first try in ruger yesterday. Mr crawley is bilding a new garige and I was carring som bricks for him at leest the hole shool was can I have a biger envlope to send this other pen in.

with love from Tudor.

Dear Mumsle,

We went to church this morning. We have grub Wedensday and Saterday. Please come down soon, because I want more grub.

I am so sorry to hear that Auntie Mildred's sister is dead. Everybody in the whole school wears vests except me, and they laugh at me, so can't I have them. The boy at the station who was going to look after me is awfully nice his name is Ebsworth and he lives in Sloane St and he is a great friend of Maxwells.

The boats were awfully nice they are a great success at this school. Please don't write any more missreble letters. I hate football, and I am awfully bad at it. I am very popular here. Our hours are from 8.45 to 7.15. Please when you come here, will you try and persuade Mr Haughtry to let Ebsworth come ouy with me, but Mr Haughtry doesn't like it.

BUT PLEASE TRY. Ebsworth's AW-FULLY nice. I have made heaps of FIRM friends. We have lovely food here. May I please have a cake on my birthday for the whole school. PLEASE will you get me some foreign stamp TO swop. Will you get some from Nannie and from Minie.

love from Peter.

Colditz Castle
POW Camp
Germany.

Dear Mummy,

Just a short letter to tell you how much I am looking forward to Tuesday, and as the boys leave to Victoria at 8.45, do you think you could come even earlier at 8.45? And tell John that if he could make it at 8.45, I would not mind him coming to collect me.

Falcon won the outing and they went to the cricket bat factory at Robertsbridge, Sussex. Is'nt it a lovely day? It is the prefect's outing.

Well, mummy I am longing for Tuesday, don't forget the Air Rifle on tuesday afternoon.

Don't forget 8.45 (quarter to nine). Give my love to Jane, John, and Prince. Write to me soon. lots and lots of love
from Guy
(Prisoner 36)

P.S. Please note address at top of letter. Don't forget 8.45.

1 p.m.

There seems to be little doubt that in the matter of the quality and quantity of the food provided, or not provided, in the less well run schools where the fees were often low, the nadir seems to have been reached between, roughly, 1916 and 1923, seven pretty bleak years. The Second World War was, on the home front, in many ways better organized than the first, the aftermath of which produced spartan conditions and poor staffs. At Stirling Court we had a gassed Major This and a limping Captain That, brave fellows to whom we owed so much then and now, in an inhospitable world, struggling away in a profession that they found both dull and profitless, in more ways than one (was it £140 p.a. that some of them got?).

It seems now almost impossible to believe but our Sunday lunch, the main meal of the day, never once varied in the four years that I was there. The menu was, I suppose, arranged to suit the convenience of the cook and the domestic staff. It consisted of two small slices of cold meat (usually mutton which I assume was cheaper and 'went further' than beef), mashed potato to which nothing whatever had been added, not even a thin dribble of milk, and cold beetroot in vinegar – not everybody's favourite vegetable. There then came those apricots, sour and uninviting, that had been, twenty-four hours before, dry, and which had spent the intervening time soaking and swelling sullenly in water. With the apricots there came a spoonful of some cold and white and moulded substance known either as blancmange (we pronounced it 'blum-monge') or 'shape', a refined sort of word.

For tea, three-and-a-half hours later, there was, but only on Sundays, one spoonful of an indifferent and unidentifiable and all-purpose jam from a vast seven-pound pot, which was eaten with bread and margarine, the meagre butter ration having been dished out for breakfast. On weekdays there was no jam except that which we provided ourselves from our tuck-boxes. If that had run out, you just made do with bread and margarine, the only solid food available between lunch and breakfast next day. A cup of extremely watery Oxo completed, at prayers, the day's intake, though occasionally a plate of dry crusts was left out for us, the crusts being scrambled for as vigorously as *sans-culottes* disputing cabbage stalks in silent films of the French Revolution. We dotted this windfall with mustard to make the pieces of bread more interesting and edible, and at bedtime the hungrier boys moodily ate (this is true) their toothpaste. Smells from calorie-packed meals being consumed on what was called 'the private side' frequently reached us and increased our hunger and general wretchedness. However, I must in honesty confess that happy snaps of one at the time reveal nothing in the way of emaciation.

As several people have pointed out, even in establishments where the food was plentiful and good, it wasn't the done thing to approve of it.

The ways of boys are past finding out, and what could have induced us to believe that the food supplied was disgusting to the verge of being

poisonous I have no idea. But tradition, at the time of which I am speaking, ordained that this was so, and how often when I was longing to eat a plateful of pudding have I shovelled it into an envelope to bury in the playground, since the currants in it were held to be squashed flies and the suet to be made with scourings from dirty plates. Then somebody once saw potatoes, no doubt intended for school consumption, lying on the floor in a shed in the garden, which was considered a terrible way in which to keep potatoes. I remember telling my father this, and with the utmost gravity he answered that every potato ought to be wrapped up singly in silver paper. He also asked if it was true that Mr Waterfield had been seen, with his trousers turned up, diluting the beer for dinner out of a garden watering-can. Most poisonous of all were supposed to be the sausages which we had for breakfast now and then; it was a point of honour not to eat a single mouthful of this garbage. Then suddenly for no reason the fashion changed, and the food was supposed to be, and indeed it probably was, excellent. We gobbled up our sausages, asked for more and got it, and ate the potatoes that had once lain on the dirty ground, and had even degraded themselves by growing in it . . .

There are exceptions to every rule and it is agreeable to be able to record a 1914–18 experience which was nutritionally superior to that of many schoolboys who have not hesitated to spill the beans.

So far as the boys were concerned, the war had little influence on the quantity and quality of the school food, which was by general consent good, plentiful and unadventurous. But their ignorance of the true state of things was bought at a price. 'Our rations were sparse; inspection visits were paid to prevent any excessive shortage of food. It was wonderful to see how many adults developed an unconquerable aversion to meat, so that the children might not go short!' For the main meal of the day there were usually great joints of beef or mutton. Thanks to the ravages of the Germans and the cabbage-whites, the vegetable diet was virtually reduced to parsnips. Stewed prunes and custard were a too-regular feature of the school lunch. On Fridays there was a sort of bread-and-butter pudding, known as Resurrection Pudding, as it was felt that everything left over during the week was put into it. It had another nickname: for forty years it was the misfortune of Mr Thwaites, a chiropodist, to make a monthly visit to inspect the boys' nails, which were cut each Thursday by the maids. The abundance of caraway seeds in Friday's pudding led to its being known as Toenail Pudding. The boys were encouraged to eat brown bread, of which the popular make was Hovis, advertised then as 'the bread that makes the butter fly'. There were frequently oranges on the breakfast tables; E.L.B. allowed the boys to take them away to eat, so long as they took care 'to put the peel in the receptacles specially provided for the purpose'. All the boys brought tuck-boxes from home, the standard plain-wood, iron-cornered boxes full of home-made jam and cakes and dates and figs and nuts and raisins and shortbread and biscuits and chocolate. If the contents of a boy's tuck-box ran out he was entitled to 'club' jam. ('Club' was a word applied to anything communal and supplied by the establishment.) The 'club' jam was army issue of plum-and-apple. It came in cardboard cylinders with a tin cap at top and bottom. To gain access to it one sawed through the cardboard at the top so as to leave a small piece intact to act as a hinge. Inside was a solid mass which had to be gouged out with a knife or spoon, and there was no juice. As far as 'drinks' were concerned, everyone was well catered for. In the cricket pavilion there were crates of lemonade, ginger beer, cherry cider and lime fizz, which the boys could help themselves to after games without any supervision. One penny per drink was paid into a cash box in the pavilion. Payment was always made. Throughout the war a good food supply was maintained, as was the stock of boiled sweets which E.L.B. kept in his study; two were awarded as a consolation prize after a boy had been thrashed.

Parents were in general totally impervious to complaints from their children about the school fare, merely greeting their wails and horror stories with, 'All I can say, dear, is that you look very well on it.' There is, however, one instance of a mother rashly writing to the headmaster to ask that a plate of sandwiches be placed nightly beside her boy's bed in case of hunger. It would help her, she added, to enjoy her own dinner more. The reactions of the headmaster, not to speak of the horrified boy, to this grave breach of school etiquette have not survived.

At one school, mealtimes furnished a pleasing musical innovation.

Lunch, shared by boarders and day-boys, was marked by the playing of records. One boy was detailed to start the gramophone, another to announce the choice of music; one piece to accompany the first course, another the second . . . the choice was not too serious. A third boy was detailed to announce the pudding. He had to leave his place, go to the middle of the room, command silence by banging on the panelling, and then proclaim 'the pudding today is . . .'

At most schools, a rather thin tea was supplied from one of those tremendously depressing urns (during the OTC uprising in that splendid anti-school film, *If*, it was cheering to see that the first rifle bullet penetrated the school urn, shooting out tea in all directions). At Stirling Court it was a firmly held belief that the urn's tea-leaves were suspended in the water in an old football stocking though, as matron presided over the contraption and permitted no meddling, it was never possible to check this.

As to the plain living, allowance must of course be made for a subject that looms disproportionately large in small boys' memories, not to mention their fertile imagination. There were even periods when convention insisted that, however wholesome the food was, it was just 'not done' to eat it . . . There was a belief that the taps on the urn, from which the housekeeper dispensed cocoa, were deliberately placed high up, so that the dregs could be made into chocolate pudding for Sunday . . . Other firmly established traditions were discarded gloves chopped up for mince-pies, the roots of weeds substituted for potatoes and, still more macabre, some

dogs' graves, which survived in a dank corner of the
grounds, were tacitly assumed to commemorate
boys for whom the diet had proved fatal.

Any supplement to the tea, bread and butter
supplied at breakfast, such as jam, sardines, or
potted meat, had to be provided from home, and
put in charge of authority. In due course they must
be shared with the rest of one's table; and soon,
when a jam jar was nearly empty, there arose a cry
of 'Bags I first scrapings!' and 'Bags I second
scrapings!' until, according to etiquette, the third
scraper was allowed to mop up the meagre residue
by pouring milk into the jar.

At most schools the fact must be faced that sympathy in a
misfortune was seldom easy to come by.

Although these formidable ladies must have spoken
to me hundreds of times I can only remember one
or two occasions at all distinctly. Once, at school
dinner, I swallowed a plumstone and was instantly
struck with terror, for like most children of that
generation I believed that any foreign body swallowed fell like a plummet into the appendix with
the most horrible consequences. I saw in a flash
my future, tragically cut short. The sequence ran
something like this: Hospital – Operation –
Collapse – Deathbed. I jumped up and hurried to
the small table where the elder principal sat alone.
'Please,' I quavered, 'I've swallowed a plumstone.'
She looked at me coldly for a moment. 'Have you
indeed?' she said. 'Go and sit down.' And that was
that.

At one school there was an ingenious method of sharing out a piece of left-over cake. The boy at the head of the table would take half the piece and then pass the remaining half to his neighbour, who in his turn halved the piece and passed on the rest, and so on round the table until what was left was almost too small to see, let alone halve.

A fine jumble of memories have been forthcoming – the between-the-wars craze for roughage-providing substances, among them the excellent product, Bemax ('Pass the sawdust'), the greasy suet puddings known to all as Dead Baby, the corned beef ('Pink Elephant'), the currant dough ('Squashed Flies'), the food swapping and barter ('Swap all your potted meat for my eggs'), the Sunday evening cocoa drinking before hymn singing, the relative absence of green vegetables and the presence of the much disliked parsnip and haricot bean, the insistence on what were called 'tidy plates' ('EAT THAT UP!'), the chocolate puddings ('Zambesi Mud'), and the way in which, no

matter what the weather or time of year, so many schools always smelt of wet linoleum and macintoshes and, even when it had not been served for weeks, cabbage.

Many would agree that they have never in their lives known such despair as that which settled on them on a prep school Sunday evening in, say, September, with the light beginning to go and the long long week and term ahead.

> To some it was sheer misery, like the home-sick new boy whose devotional innocence I hope I may be forgiven for quoting;

>> 'Dearest Mother, this is awful,
>> Come and take me home at once,
>> For Jesus Christ's sake, Amen.'

2 p.m.

While penning his immortal tale, *Eric ; Or, Little by Little,*
the excellent Dean Farrar, at one time headmaster of
Marlborough, made use of a neat literary device. 'I hurry
over a part of my subject inconceivably painful,' he writes,
the subject in question being indecent talk in the dormitory
by a degraded boy 'of feeble intellect' called Ball. Then,
steeling himself for the hateful task, our author adds, having
after all decided to have it both ways, 'I hurry over it, but
if I am to perform my self-imposed duty of giving a true
picture of what school life *sometimes* is, I must not pass by
it altogether.' No indeed. Those who may wish to know
what indecencies deplorable Ball came out with (Eric, as
you'll recall, 'blushed scarlet to the roots of his hair') must
be disappointed, for Dean Farrar is too appalled to pass
them on to us. We can, however, allow ourselves a con-
jecture as to exactly what Freudian urge nudged our author
into choosing that particular surname for his culprit.

Our subject here is not indecent talk but flogging, beating, caning, swishing, call it what you will, and there is no
hurrying over it, however 'inconceivably painful' (to the
floggees, mostly) it may be. We cannot hurry because in
many of our ex-schoolboys' minds it is the subject of

flogging that looms largest, even taking precedence over food (inadequacy of), games, work and absence of *de luxe* living.

Let us begin with a characteristic example of the kind of thing that went on.

There was a tremendous amount of official beating. The head was a devout believer in the efficacy of cane and slipper. He did not beat boys particularly hard, but he beat them perpetually. He beat them for quite minor misdemeanours and he beat them for doing nothing at all. There was a great deal of talking after 'lights out'. Quite rightly, the head wanted to stop this – although he was psychologically incapable of understanding that allowing children to talk, perhaps for ten minutes, would be regarded as a privilege which would not be abused. Instead, the head crept about the place in tennis shoes, like a cat burglar. When he pounced on a dormitory, he expected the talkers to 'own up' at once; if they did not, all the boys in the dormitory were beaten.

This was insane. Small boys, still asleep, were lugged from their beds and told to bend over. The trouble-makers were usually the biggest boys, who were the least tired after the Spartan day of work and games. They were generally not in the least bit conscience-stricken by getting others beaten too; they regarded this, in fact, as a good joke. Beating, if intended to be a real deterrent, should be carried out as seldom as possible. When it becomes routine, it's worse than useless.

Beatings in prep schools were always administered 'after'

something: 'Come and see me after Fire Drill': 'I want to see the following in my study after tea': 'Partridge and Courtney are to report to Mr Millcroft after supper'. It can be argued that any event in the scholastic day must needs be after something, but here the 'after' often meant hours of apprehension and an agonizing wait while the horrors ahead magnified themselves in the mind.

The 'old man' himself wielded the big stick moderately frequently. There seems something positively indecent in a man of about sixty beating a small boy with a bamboo cane. It was not perhaps so much the physical act itself as the intense drama with which the whole thing was invested that condemned the practice of corporal punishment. It was the cultivated horror of 'waiting till after prayers' that was so wrong, the macabre juxtaposition of compulsory religion alongside a deliberately delayed vengeance. I don't suppose he in fact hit particularly hard, yet the bruises that were sometimes proudly displayed afterwards would have been difficult to discount as evidence of assault in a court of law. Six strokes were regarded as a severe punishment and I shall never forget the look of disillusioned horror on the face of one boy as he returned from receiving this award. That he had been able to suffer it without physical collapse was reason enough for him to be hero worshipped as a martyr, and the fact that he had to wait some hours to receive it (with all the school aware of its imminence) gave the whole place something of the atmosphere of a prison on the eve of an execution. Thus was the prep school larger than life, yet smaller.

The later in the day that retribution came, the worse it was and some sad cases of real sadism and cruelty have come to light. There was the small boy of nine who, caught committing some punishable crime, was told by the headmaster (a clergyman, I fear) that he would be 'dealt with' later in the day. The hours dragged by and nothing happened. Supper and prayers came and went with no summons to the study. The bedtime bell was rung and soon the whole school was in bed, with the headmaster and his wife making their usual round of the dormitories. They were particularly agreeable to the nine-year-old and the dormitory door was just closing, to cries of 'Goodnight, Mrs Robins, goodnight, sir' when it was gently opened again and the quietly smiling headmaster returned. 'Ah,' he said, and over the years one can almost hear the odious relish in the way the word was uttered, 'but we're forgetting something, aren't we?' And the culprit was removed from bed, taken downstairs and soundly beaten. This sort of thing turns the stomach.

What were considered to be offences and what were considered to be appropriate correctives for such offences varied greatly from place to place. At one school of my acquaintance, almost the worst crime of the lot, apart, I suppose, from trying to achieve an indecency with the headmaster's wife, was to go out of doors, even if the day were dry and sunny, wearing your house-shoes. Doubt and pitfalls were everywhere.

> The punishments were very unexpected and curious. One boy was suddenly flogged for cutting off a piece of his hair and keeping the piece in his drawer. In the second division the boys were punished by electricity. The division was made to

join hands, and a strong electric shock was passed through it. This went on until one day one boy, smarting from an overcharge of electricity, took the battery and threw it at the master's head, inflicting a sharp wound. Nothing was said about this action, to the immense astonishment of the boys, who thought it jolly of him not to sneak.

The Black Book of a very celebrated school contains a finely varied list of actions that plainly ranked as punishable:

'Deliberately walking into a snowdrift in his ordinary clothes'
'Describing a cricket ball as bloody'
'Played with milk in prep after warnings'
'Being dangerous with lino-work tools'
'Trying to take two buns'
'Misbehaviour with a razor-blade'
'Bringing comics into chapel'
'Wearing another boy's shorts'
'Rebellion against prefects'
'Banging a boy's head on the floor'

At Stirling Court a rebellion against the prefects was unthinkable, for they possessed completely despotic powers. It will hardly be believed but when I went there, aged nine, in 1920, they had the authority to beat. There were six of them, they were each aged thirteen, they called themselves the Star Chamber and they plainly thought the cane (in old-fashioned advertisements of scholastic requirements – desks, chalk, blackboards, etc – canes are tastefully described as Young Gentlemen's Correction Switches) far too feeble an instrument. The school lay near a wartime seaplane base where broken and disused parts of aeroplanes abounded, among them long lengths of inch-thick rubber

which, I suppose, formed part of the under-carriage's shock-absorbers. A three-foot length of this rubber made an alarming and fearfully painful alternative to the correction switch and one came to dread the regular summons to the bathroom where these executions took place. I was once beaten for having a dirty neck. They then tried to wash my neck, only to discover that the dirt wasn't dirt at all but sunburn. Eventually somebody blabbed to his parents and the Star Chamber was dissolved and the beating privilege withdrawn.

It is no exaggeration to say that some boys spent their school lives in a constant state of fear.

On Monday morning there was a dreadful ordeal called Reading Over. The headmaster, arrayed in a silk gown, used to descend from an upper-floor staircase which was hidden from view by a red curtain stamped with black *fleurs-de-lis* and stand at his desk; on his right sat two masters, on his left sat two others, in gowns. In front of him the whole school were assembled on chairs. Each division was called up in turn and stood in the order of the last week's marks; they changed their places as the marks were read out, according to the variation of the week. Thus, sometimes, a boy who had been nearly at the top would go down nearly to the bottom. Then the comments on the boys' work were made by each division master, and any striking events of the week were read out by the headmaster. And if one had done anything bad it was now that it came to light. If it was very bad the boy was told that he would be severely punished: this meant flogging with a birch, which took place in the headmaster's sitting-room over a block on

which a hairy rug was stretched. The headmaster
fortified himself for the execution by first drinking
a glass of Marsala. At the time, the boys took these
floggings as a matter of course, but it has been put
on record by boys who were at this school, and who
have since attained the age of reason, and some of
them to positions of importance, that these floggings were exceedingly severe.

This Monday morning ordeal was a permanent
shadow, for the boys lived for the greater part in
complete uncertainty, never knowing whether they
had or not committed some terrible crime; for some
of the worst crimes were unexpected, such as
spoken or implied criticism of the food, to speak to
another boy if you met him outside the school
during school hours, to have missed getting the
message telling you to stop talking at meals, to turn
on the electric light, to eat any food, even a grape,
if brought by your parents. And it was a curious
fact that the boy was sometimes quite unaware
until Monday morning arrived that he had committed any offence.

Whether punishment on the hand is more effective and
painful than elsewhere is a moot point.

By far the most salient feature in the school, even as
the sun is the most salient feature in the day,
making it precisely what it is, was Mr Waterfield
himself. He seems now to me to have been nine
feet high, and he certainly walked with a curious
rocking motion, which was convenient, because if
you were where you should not be, you could
detect his coming long before he could detect any-

body. He had a square grey beard which smelt of cigars, a fact known from his practice, when he had frightened the life out of you by terrible harangues, of saying, 'Well, that's all over my boy,' and kissing you. I believe him to have been about the best private schoolmaster who ever lived, for he ruled by love and fear combined in a manner that, while it inspired small boys with hellish terror, yet rewarded them with the sweet fruits of hero-worship. He exacted blind obedience, under peril of really infamous torture with a thick ruler with which he savagely caned offending hands, but he managed at the same time to make us appreciate his approbation. The ruler was kept in a convenient drawer of the kneehole table in his study, and was a perfectly brutal instrument, but the approach of the ruler, like a depression over the Atlantic, was always heralded by storm-cones. The first of these was the taking of the keys from his trousers-pocket, and then you had time to pull yourself together to retract an equivocation, to confess a fault, or try to remember something you had been repeatedly told. The second storm-cone was the insertion of the key into the drawer where the ruler was kept. You had to be of very strong nerve when that second storm-cone was hoisted, and divert your mind from the possible future to the supine which you could not recollect, for when the key was once inserted there might any moment be a sudden startling explosion of wrath, and out flew the ruler. Then came a short agonizing scene, and the blubbering victim after six smart blows had the handle of the door turned for him by somebody else, because his hands were useless through pain. The ruler was quite rare, and probably well deserved; anyhow it was the counter-balance to the hero-worship born of Mr Waterfield's approval. For more heinous offences there was birching, but that had certain compensations, for afterwards you took down your breeches and showed the injured parts to admiring companions. But there was nothing to show, as Mrs Pullet said about the boluses, when you were caned. Besides you could play cricket quite easily, shortly after a whipping, but no human hand could hold a bat shortly after the application of the ruler.

To the pain and indignity of corporal punishment there was once an additional discomfiture. At a southern Choir School, the headmaster's daughter, a sadly bloodthirsty girl who devoted herself to culinary duties, was accustomed, on hearing her father belabouring somebody, to rattle open the window between the kitchen and the schoolroom and shout encouragement; 'That's right, Father; very glad it's him. Give it him well.'

To redress the balance, let us remember that in the same school, the boy who acted as deputy organ blower was also something of a poet and threw off, during a short respite from the bellows, an 'Ode to the Bishop's Throne', an ode of which the following are the closing lines:

Great Burgess too! What man so fit
Beneath my purple dome to sit?
To grace thy seat long may he live
And Heaven's choicest gifts receive;
And when – Oh Heav'n avert the day!
His aged form shall turn to clay,
May angels hover round his head

T'receive his soul when it is fled:
And may He who of all sin the scourge is
Grant thou may'st always hold a man like
Burgess!

While admiring the neat rhyme for Burgess, let us hasten to say that the gentleman thus addressed is, of course, the good Bishop Burgess, a saintly figure who handed out for Christmas signed copies of his own 'Catechisms', the surname of Burgess having fallen, in recent years, into disrepute.

Schoolmasters who have always found it distasteful to beat and personally inflict pain will be interested to learn of a way out of this dilemma when a beating is necessary. The name of the cricketer, W. G. Grace, is famous yet and lives on, but the name of his great-uncle, Alfred Pocock, is less well known. It was he, however, who was a schoolmaster and who invented an ingenious beating machine. It was presumably, for the year was 1854, steam-driven, it had a dial which could be set to the number of whacks and their strength, and it was impervious to screams. The sensitive punisher retired to his study and played no further part in the proceedings.

In addition to the actual pain of caning, a public humiliation was sometimes considered to be a valuable added corrective.

My only lasting success at Sandroyd was achieved in my final term when I got a public beating. In all my five years there nothing like this had ever happened. Matron, who rejoiced in the name of Sister Cowe – we were told she came from Berwick-on-Tweed – frequently spanked us with slippers, or Mason & Pearson hairbrushes, in the privacy of the dormitory; but a public caning was unheard of. So to be the first to receive one in my generation was a unique distinction. The reason for it was 'Ma Brown'. Ma Brown kept a sweet shop on the edge of Oxshott woods, which we used to pass every Sunday on our strictly supervised walks. She kept the most delicious sweets, including, delight of delights, the newly invented Mars Bar. At school we were only allowed 2d worth of mixed sweets sent down from Harrods, which were issued by the Rev. J. E. Langdon (known as Bunch) on Saturdays. By the end of the cricket match they had all gone, and come Monday one was yearning for sweets as a drug addict for heroin. One of my contemporaries bet me I would not dare to go to Ma Brown's and buy four Mars Bars.

So on Wednesday afternoon (half-holiday and another cricket match) I crept away to Ma Brown's. Unhappily, on my return I ran slap bang into Priscilla, one of the two mistresses at the school, who taught Latin to the eight-year-olds (it was from her that I learnt to address tables and walls in the second person singular, 'O table, O wall' and have found it most useful ever since) and was engaged in order to give us a feeling of 'home' when we first arrived. I trusted Priscilla and got on with her quite well, but this stood me in no good stead; she reported me to the HM.

That evening in chapel, after the grace of the Lord Jesus and the Love of God had been evoked upon our young heads, there was an ominous hush. I was summoned to appear forthwith in the assembly room; I am rather surprised now that it wasn't in front of the altar. And there, before the whole school and all the staff, my shorts were lowered, I bent over and received ten of the best. From that moment, until I left six weeks later, I was the hero of the school.

Two achievements, both worthy of being included in the Guinness Book of Records, must be noted: one a notable instance of Pluck, another a remarkable feat of Strength and Endurance.

There was a good bit of beating, particularly for talking after lights out, and punishment was usually administered in the dormitory before breakfast, by means of a cane on the palm of the hand. Those of us who were cast in the role of dormitory story-tellers (made up ghost stories were especially favoured) became quite used to the cane. We had one bad patch with a beast of a master who chose to administer beatings on the bare bottom at bath time, but he was eventually sacked after a parent discovered the barely healed wounds during the holidays.

Other highlights were the public beating of a senior boy, who had been stealing chocolate from a school tuck cupboard (he fought back and was eventually subdued by the combined staff and put to bed with a swollen nose and two teeth missing).

I attended an excellent prep school from 1964–1969. The school was run by a headmaster who was, without doubt, a success academically and was responsible more than anyone else there for making it such a very good school. However, much of his academic success was a result of a particularly vicious and sarcastic tongue which goaded us into our various public schools; the rest

came from his cane which was produced with monotonous regularity. One day the whole school (a hundred and eight of us) were having our elevenses, which consisted of a small bottle of milk and a straw, and half a slice of margarine and marmite. For some reasons best known to themselves the prefects decided that elevenses were to be a silent affair. 'Shut up,' they yelled, but to no avail. Unfortunately the head was correcting an LGP (Latin Grammar Paper) upstairs and this had been very poorly attempted by some luckless form. He stormed down to us, told the head boy to fetch his cane, and announced that he would beat the whole school apart from the prefects, in order to teach us to do as we were told. What did rather surprise us was that he proceeded to give all ninety-eight of us three of the best each. I have never come across anyone whose headmaster beat the whole of such a large school – I wonder if this is unique?

Those who imagine that there has never been a lighter side to corporal punishment are wrong, as this merry incident shows.

In the common room one morning the headmaster reported an occasion when corporal punishment meted out by him had been 'hardly as dreadful as it ought to be'. He had found it necessary to correct, with the aid of a slipper, a tendency by one dormitory to become noisily conversational before the first gong. Finding the proceedings somewhat lengthy and pausing to take stock and rest his arm he had discovered that each victim had rejoined the queue and was coming round again for further correction.

Canings and beatings and whack-whack-whack in general echo down the years. A future brigadier remembers being firmly held down by four other boys during a birching, a Latin Grammar being placed between his teeth to help the culprit to manage a manly silence. There was the boy who was punished (three in his pyjamas) for not saying his prayers for long enough. And another bedtime produced a mêlée of a surprising nature.

A new boy arrived from Spain and Mr Reading, the house tutor, showed him round the school before taking him to the dormitory where he was to sleep. There were eight of us in the dorm at the time and I was head of the dorm. At nine o'clock it was bedtime and we all got undressed and put on our pyjamas, except for the new boy. At ten o'clock it was lights out and Mr Reading came into the dormitory to see if everybody was asleep. No one was and, when he saw the new boy still fully dressed, his eyes nearly popped out. He asked the boy to take off his clothes. 'No,' answered the boy softly. Mr Reading called for the matron and she came in: 'Undress that boy!' It was easier said than done; his socks, shirt and tie were easy to get off, but when she tried to get off his shorts she had another think coming. He kicked, punched and yelled for help and some Spanish words came out. I think he was calling for his mother, but I wasn't sure.

The prefect outside the door came in to give a hand. The matron and the new boy were on the floor by this time. Being in bed we couldn't see all that was going on, but we heard a lot as instructions were given to the prefect. He held the boy's legs,

Mr Reading held his arms. At last matron had got
his pants off and his pyjamas on and he was in bed.
For some nights after that he struggled to get his
pants off and his pyjamas on while wrapped in a
big towel, but eventually he became used to us.

Here is a final example of apprehension, pain and cruelty
before we pass on to more jocund matters.

After evening benediction every term, every day
except Sunday we filed out of chapel for supper.
The prefects and their deputies dropped out of
line and went into the senior classroom to compose
The List.

Many of us were unable to eat in the sheer agony
of anticipation that we could be on that fatal list.
The food was terrible and we were always hungry.
At top-table the headmaster sat between his
assistant and a lay master. Their food was excellent.
We, below the salt, were given watery cocoa in
winter, frizzled kippers or dead fish-cakes on
Fridays – on Wednesdays as well during Lent;
watery scrambled eggs or mince equally watery and
often thick greasy, scalding soup and of course,
carefully counted slices of bread and margarine.
In summer we did have lemonade – of the rather
nice vicarage garden-party variety. But there was
always The List.

After a time the prefects came into the refectory.
They took their places one at the head of each
table and some answered our query, 'Am I on The
List?', with a gleeful nod or sullen shake of the
head. Others gave a glassy stare at such an insolent
question. The head prefect put The List, folded in

half, beside the HM's plate and went to his own place, aloof, superior, and quite unapproachable.

Two knocks by the HM with a knife-handle brought us to our feet to recite our thanks for food received and the rest in peace of the faithful departed – whom, at that moment we envied. This was followed by the chilling announcement, 'I will see these boys in my study.' He then read out the names on The List and left the refectory followed by his staff.

We hurriedly clattered up the brass-nosed, lino-covered back stairs over the boot-hole.(!) The front staircase was out of bounds to all boys at all times. We made our way to the headmaster's corridor with its hideous red Turkey carpet and waited bleakly in two facing lines on either side of his black painted door. It seemed an eternity before we heard the tell-tale creak of a loose floorboard which heralded 'The Coming'. The HM usually enjoyed an after-supper cigarette or pipe with his assistant downstairs, and so we waited. He looked neither right nor left as he passed between us. The only sound was made by his cassock whipping round his heels as he walked to the door which he opened and closed firmly behind him. A familiar and frightening smell of leather and tobacco assailed our quivering nostrils – the intimidating odour of masculine strength and power.

After a few trembling seconds, the first boy knocked gingerly. 'Come in,' came a fearsome voice, and in he went. Thick as that black door was, heavy and full the dingy green chenille curtain behind it to exclude draughts, whose brass rod squealed in pro-test at each opening and shutting, we could still hear blood-freezing sounds, which although muffled, were, nonetheless, distinct enough for us to know exactly what was happening within. A bass voice gave question and command, a tiny treble piped reply. Then came the sickening thwack and thud of the 'Paddycock'. The punishment strokes varied in number only – one on each – two on each – three on each – and sometimes, six on each. We often swopped places to be last in line.

When I went in, as with the others before me, the ritual was identical. 'You're on The List.' 'Yes, sir.' 'Pull up your sleeves. Open your hands. Keep your thumbs straight out against your fingers.' Then came the vicious pain from this evil contraption, The 'Paddycock', comprised of an elongated oval of leather about three eighths of an inch thick, over a foot long, very flexible and attached to a short wooden handle. The HM grasped the handle in his right hand while he controlled the end of the leather oval in his left. He then raised both arms to shoulder height releasing the tongue as his right arm descended. The tough leather smacked hard down on the flat open hand. The recipient held up and lowered each hand alternately to receive the number of strokes allotted. Because of the pulled up sleeves the tip of that wicked tongue invariably stung the tenderer inside of the wrists as well. Some boys believed that two hairs pulled from the head, each hand clutching one before going in, would be invisible to the HM and would lessen the pain. It didn't. Anyway the first thwack blew the hairs off.

2.30 p.m.

There may well be schools nowadays where participation in formal games of football (both varieties) and cricket is no longer compulsory, provided that exercise of some sort (fives or tennis or swimming or, in fortunate cases, sailing) is taken, for exercise will ever be thought to promote that smooth functioning of the internal organs to which we have already referred, though nobody seems to have wondered how we managed to get through the holidays without clogging permanently up. A few years ago, however, it would have been as unthinkable to be able to avoid cricket and football as it would have been to avoid work. In those days, the only respite from the two tyrannies was provided by rain.

When inclement weather had made the playing fields too sodden for games, other forms of physical exercise were resorted to. 'One other memory (a mystery) comes to mind. We had been sent on a run. One boy, a very fine runner, got bored with our slow pace and made a détour which brought him to a little stream containing frogspawn. Apparently he ate large quantities, and not surprisingly became ill that evening. He was never seen or heard of again. Several boarders assured us they had seen a hearse call next day.' The provider of this information emphasizes the excellence of the school where this bizarre substitute for tasty tapioca occurred.

From time to time in the summer term cricket matches were played against other schools. Away games required the presence of a *char-à-banc*, or the more modern coach or fleet of masters' cars, to transport the gifted players to their match, and on their return it was the done thing, if they had been able to win, to cheer themselves loudly on entering the school grounds, the rest of the school loyally joining in. Who knows, it might mean an extra half holiday.

From home matches, there was no escape. The whole school was instructed to sit and watch and, if occasion allowed, applaud, an instruction which some obeyed more zealously than others.

One day we were looking on at a cricket match which was being played against another school. The school was getting beaten, the day was hot, the match was long and tedious, and Broadwood and another boy called Bell and myself wandered away from the match and two of us climbed up the wooden platform, which was used for letting off fireworks on the 5th of November. Bell remained below, and we threw horse-chestnuts at him, which he caught in his mouth.

Presently one of the masters advanced towards us, biting his knuckles, which he did when he was in a great rage, and glowered. He ordered us indoors, and gave us two hours' work to do in the third division schoolroom. We went in as happy as larks and glad to be in the cool. But at tea we saw there was something seriously amiss. The rival eleven who had beaten us were present, but not a word was spoken. There was an atmosphere of impending doom over the school charged with the thunder of a coming row. After tea, when the guests had gone, the school was summoned into the hall, and the head, gowned and frowning, addressed us and accused the whole school in general, and Broadwood, Bell and myself in particular, of want of patriotism, bad manners, inattention, and vulgarity. He was disgusted, he said, with the behaviour of the school before strangers. We were especially guilty, but the whole school had shown want of attention, and gross callousness and in-difference to the cricket match (which was all too true) and consequently had tarnished the honour of the school. There was to have been an expedition to the New Forest next week. That expedition would not come off; in fact, it would never come off. And the speech ended and the school trooped out in gloomy silence and broke up into furtive whispering groups.

That night in my cubicle I said to Worthington that I thought Campbell minor, who had been scoring during the match, had certainly behaved well all day, and didn't he deserve to go to the New Forest? 'No,' said Worthington, 'he whistled twice.' 'Oh,' I said, 'then of course he can't go.'

The basic difference between cricket and football and other sporting activities is well summed up in the following fairly painful memory.

After luncheon we played prisoner's base, and I at once realized that there is a vast difference between games and play. Play is played for fun but games are deadly serious, and you do not play them to

enjoy yourselves. Everyone was given two blue
cards and every time you were taken prisoner you
lost a card. If you lost both you were kicked by the
captain of the side, who said we were a pack of
dummies.

In the afternoons we played Rugby football, an
experience which was in my case exactly what Max
Beerbohm describes it in one of his Essays : running
about on the edge of a muddy field. The second
division master pursued the players with exhorta-
tions and imprecations, and every now and then a
good kicking was administered to the less successful
and energetic players, of which there were quite a
number. The three best rugby football players
were allowed to wear on Sundays a light blue velvet
cap with a silver Maltese cross on it, and a silver
tassel. I am sorry to say that this cap was not always
given to the best players. It was given to the boys
the headmaster liked best.

Boxing is now rightly regarded as a dangerous activity but
years ago the school authorities felt no apprehension and
all were forced to box. Boxing was manly and, in the empire,
straight lefts were greatly admired and often proved an
effective way of showing some foreigner that he was wrong.
Boxing, gymnastics and what were once all too accurately
known as physical jerks took place in the gym and under
the supervision, usually, of a crimson-faced ex-Army
sergeant with a chest like a pouter pigeon. Happily recalled
are those cries of ''Ands on yer 'ips and 'op 'op 'op.'

We were taught to box and unfortunately I earned,
by mistake, the reputation of being a 'killer'.
Nothing could be more untrue than to say that I

'packed a punch', indeed I was a rather weedy lad with little in the shape of muscles in my arms. My opponent must have fallen forward and struck his nose on my glove just as he was about to have a super nose bleed. He had to be led away to the sick quarters gushing gore, while I was banned from boxing with anyone except the sergeant-instructor. He was a cocky little man who, with his guard down, used to weave to and fro in front of me crying 'Hit me on the nose, sir, hit me on the nose.' He also impressed on us that the golden rule in boxing was to watch your opponent's eyes, which would be looking direct at the spot he intended to strike. I wondered whether this was an infallible rule so, to try it out, I looked intently at his stomach and then hit him square on the nose. I expect that this hurt his pride rather more than his nose.

Stirling Court being on the Solent, which rejoices in two tides a day, one of which was always suitable to our time-table, a daily swim in the summer term did at least cut down on the time available for cricket or boxing. After we had had our bathe (icy-cold water and pebbly beach) and were trying to dry ourselves on seldom very dry towels, a large and beefy master used to give show-off swimming demonstrations, his 'dolphin' and 'porpoise' aquatic antics being much admired and received, if we were in the mood, with applause. A request to imitate a German submarine was considered to be impertinent and the requester (Williamson) was punished.

As we swam and larked about in the shallows, ocean liners were to be seen steaming down Southampton Water and rounding The Needles, on their way to exotic places and carrying, doubtless, exotic persons. One imagined the decks to be crowded with such as Gladys Cooper, Carpentier, Nellie Melba and the Aga Khan, all cheerily playing shuffle-board or quoits and drinking champagne, and one longed to be part of the fun. One longed, in fact, for almost anything that didn't happen to be Stirling Court.

At other times, sea-planes buzzed to and fro and a great fuss was made about the Schneider Trophy, the race being centred on the Isle of Wight. Work and cricket were abandoned for the day and we repaired, with our rugs, to the cliff top and a grandstand view. The aircraft seemed to be going at a really tremendous speed (by 1931 it was 340 m.p.h., so I suppose that way back in 1924 it would have been about 200 m.p.h.) and the whole day was exhilarating.

At our Eastbourne establishment there was an admirably robust attitude to bathing.

> Swimming took place all the year round. Sea-bathes were not unbridled romps. Only a doctor's certificate excused a boy from his swim, and on occasions some fortitude was required to brave the angry rollers which broke over the reef. If the tide was coming in while the boys were dressing in the bathing-machines, an elderly horse was harnessed to each machine in turn and dragged it up the shingle, with some resulting chaos within. There was no lying or sunning on the beach in those days, by bathers of either sex, and E.L.B. forbade shouting during bathes, 'lest a cry for help should go unheard'.

> When the sea became too cold, the boys went in a cloud of bicycles down the dusty road to the Devonshire Baths, where they were coached in diving and swimming, learning the recently adopted 'crawl' stroke. All the boys were expected to slide down the

chute into the pool. It mattered not in the least to
E.L.B. that a boy might not be able to swim: he
was loudly told to put his trust in God and in the
master swimming about at the bottom of the chute.
Once, Sergeant Jefferies, who liked the boys to
think he was fierce and impressive, was treading
water when a boy came down the chute and landed
on his head, knocking him out. Ornate swimming
certificates were won at the Devonshire Baths, and
at the end of the winter term the school swimming
sports took place over three days. Among the
meticulously catalogued results of 1911 there is a
sad little entry:

Senior Swimming Race: Heat 2
1. Veitch
2. Muir
3. Rayson
4. Skinner
5. de Pass

Pearson lost his false tooth and did not finish.

No account of swimming at St Andrew's would be
anywhere near complete without a mention of the
'plunge bath', which was built at the turn of the
century. Although E.L.B. admitted that it was
matribus detestata, he was proud of it. A tiled room
housed the bath, which was about fourteen feet
long, six feet wide and nearly six feet deep. Steps
and bricks set into one wall served as rudimentary
diving platforms. First thing every morning the
boys were obliged to leap into its invigorating icy
waters. E.L.B. put coins at the bottom of the bath
to encourage the divers, and it was in the 'plunge'
that he taught generations of St Andrew's boys to

swim. After he had mastered the basic strokes lying over a piano stool, the boy would be put in a rubber ring on the end of a broomstick-fishing-line and trawled up and down the bath. Then E.L.B., crying 'Now swim for it!', would command the boy to jump into the bath and fend for himself. He held the ring just out of the boy's reach. Nobody drowned.

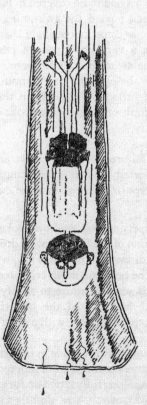

Once again, public humiliation was an effective way of encouraging those who could not swim, to swim.

> The school cap, worn on the back of the head, was dark blue or black, not much bigger than a skull cap with a very small peak and a blue silk badge showing the white eagle which was the crest of the school. On the top of the cap was the usual small button and this had to be covered in light blue until its wearer had passed the swimming test. Not to have done so became increasingly shaming and the scheme was a very good way of persuading the laggard. The swimming baths were at the side of the Ouse, in the open air and without any form of heating and little protection from the wind. The test was a simple one and breast stroke was favoured by the majority.

Successes and failures at both cricket and football were relentlessly reported, and at great length, in the school magazine, the reporters being, in some cases, merciless in criticism.

> It is not surprising that the boys looked forward to the publication of the *Gazette* with dread, and I can still see the drawn face of Keats mi., with his rather bushy hair, he being no mean cricketer, reading the record of his weekly failure to satisfy the experts, and how he had funked the ball (BALL being printed in capital letters), with a stoic pallor.

Occasionally muddles were made in the arranging of cricket and football fixtures and it is remembered that one school First XI, bowling along fully kitted up for what they thought was to be an away match, was slightly taken aback to see their opponents, similarly attired, motoring swiftly past them in the opposite direction. Both teams then waited for the other at journey's end, and the match was cancelled.

Difficulties arose in cases where a school of, say, two hundred boys was due to play against a school of about sixty.

> In football and cricket the school tended to win rather more than three-quarters of its matches at first team level. The senior teams would play anything up to twenty matches a season, and after a while it became quite common to field eight elevens simultaneously. The lowlier teams were not always so successful as their elders and betters, but the games master of another prep school once wrote to E.L.B.:
>
> I think if our second plays your 5th, or 4th at the most, we shall not have such a foolish game.
>
> Our 2nd is not, in the ordinary sense of the word, a football team; it plays its own game, and none of us quite knows what to call it. The team uses the conventional ball, but in matches only half the ground. Generally their opponents don't trouble to have goalposts, as ours are the only ones needed. In refereeing you bring a chair and sit down beside our goalkeeper, for that is where the true fight goes on. This lot played . . . II to start with and did not win by 9–0. So I said, 'Let's have . . . III,' and it was so. Then the match came off, and we did not win by 6–0.
>
> It really is beastly dangerous for the backs of the other side, standing about in the damp or cold weather with those short knickers on. The only sensible thing I can think of is for us to defend

wickets instead of goalposts, and when the football
is fairly kicked and knocks the bails off you have
one goal.

I'm sorry to be again taking a pessimist's view of
our football. I don't see anything to cheer me. Our
boys seem pretty fair at marbles and stamps – I
don't know if we could arrange a game.

Readers may be somewhat surprised to read the following:

The third XV in 1922 included a certain L.
Cochrane at centre three-quarter. The report of
the game said, 'Lesbia quite justified her selection,
especially as a safe tackle,' and in the return match
at home, 'Lesbia got a neat try after a capital run
and pass by John Walsham.'

The report is from the Dragon School, first in so many
ways and here anticipating by many years the present-day
bias towards co-education.

Quite often, in the summer months particularly, games
were dropped in favour of an expedition. At Stirling Court
a *char-à-banc*, a conveyance vulgarly known as a 'chara',
was periodically ordered to take the whole school to the
cricket ground at Portsmouth where the Hampshire XI
was involved in some needle match. For some of us, watching cricket was less frightful than actually playing it,
though it is a debatable point. We took sandwiches with us
and purchased at the ground endless bottles of fizzy
lemonade. The more daring boys left the ground for a stroll
in the town, and three of them were once sufficiently
enterprising to have tea in Fuller's (spotted by authority
and beaten, naturally, on their return to school).

A visit to a cricket ground hardly ranks as an expedition,

the following being good examples of the real thing.

> I left this school at the end of four terms, my ex-
> perience the richer from having seen Huntley &
> Palmer's factory; the Great Western Works; the
> Tower of London; and Shanklin, Isle of Wight.

Expeditions made excellent material for the school magazine, not a detail of the treat being omitted.

> There was a school magazine called the *Gazette*,
> and in it the boys used to write accounts of these
> expeditions. They always did this in collaboration.
> It took two or three, and sometimes four, boys to
> write the shortest account of the shortest expedition.
> Here is an account of one, transcribed word for
> word from the school *Gazette* (only the names have
> been altered):

> Today the head and the first division went for an
> expedition to Sidmouth, in south Devon. We
> started by the 8.53 train, and met the head and
> Huxley ma. at Basingstoke. We had our dinner in
> the train, and arrived at Sidmouth at 1.5. We then
> took a bus to the Royal York Hotel, where we left
> our luggage. We then went round a little point, and
> there we bathed, which we enjoyed very much. We
> returned round the point and got a boat. We then
> fished, but without any signal success. When we
> turned back again, Darwin ma. was violently sick,
> but he soon recovered. When we got to the shore
> we went to see the life-boat, which one of the
> coast guards showed us. It was, he said, a very large
> one. Afterwards we went into the town, and then
> went back to the Royal York Hotel and had our tea,

which consisted of mackerel and eggs. The people
at the hotel had kindly engaged a drag to take us to
the station. When we got to the station some boys
got on the engine, the engine-driver kindly allowing
them to, till we got to Sidmouth Junction, where
they got off. After waiting a few minutes there, we
got into the train and went straight to Vauxhall,
where we got out and caught the train which reached
Windsor at 1.10 a.m. We found our flys waiting for
us. We got to Ascot at about 2.20 a.m. Then when
we had had some soup in the kitchen we went to
bed just as it was beginning to get light, after having
spent a most enjoyable day (and night).

Expeditions involved, of course, extra expense and here
the schools with higher fees got about more than the others.

These expeditions played a constant and an important part in our lives; almost every week there
was a small expedition of some kind. On Ascension
Day, the whole school would be taken for an expedition – perhaps to Frimley; and once a year the
choir had an expedition of their own, which was far
more complicated and adventurous than any of the
others, because we went farther afield by train; it
was far more than a picnic, it was a Cook's tour. I
think if that headmaster had been alive today the
choir expedition would have gone to Moscow or
Rome by air and back in the same day.

'What a wonderful school!' you will say; 'what
an enlightened, what an advanced, what a modern
headmaster! The school must have been a fore-
runner of Oundle.'

4 p.m.

With games safely over and prep merely a distant prospect
eighty minutes away (a lifetime at that age) and there being
for the moment no risk of a caning (nobody was, for some
reason, ever summoned for a beating 'after cricket' or 'after
football', activities considered holier than religious ones),
4 p.m. or so was a happy restful time devoted to assorted
hobbies and pastimes and indoor and unorganized games,
with the sound of a bouncing ping-pong ball never very
far away (can it be true, as some claim, that the Italian for
ping-pong is pinka-ponka?).

Before passing on to a review of the more ordinary
pursuits, here is the record of a splendidly enterprising
spare time achievement. I only hope that its executant won
some coveted individual prize or cup, the Pendlebury
Chalice for Initiative perhaps, the sort of trophy always
awarded in school stories to those who rescue under-
matrons from the mill-race, opportunities now denied to
many by under-matrons' unfortunate ability to swim.

Finding a mother duck sitting on a nest one boy
borrowed one of her seven eggs and proceeded to
carry it around with him, night and day, tucked
under an armpit, with occasional help from one or
two friends. Towards the end of lunch one day he

approached the master at the end of his table and said, 'Please, sir, can I leave the room, I think I've hatched a duck!' And presently, with a junior matron acting as midwife, and hot milk supplied from the kitchen, the number of boarders was duly increased by one duckling.

In the more expensive, though not necessarily scholastically better, schools there was frequently a shallow concrete pool for sailing boats, model ones naturally; also, even more enjoyable and indoors, a large permanently laid-out model train track, complete with embankments and steep gradients and, in an unearthly bright green colour, rather unreal miniature bushes dotted here and there.

At Field Place we had a model train room with a large gauge O track, on which the boys were able to run their own Hornby and other locomotives and trains. Many of these railway sets were very lavish and contained stations, points, tunnels, signals etc. The engines and carriages were all in their correct livery, so that a GWR train like the 'Torbay Limited' or the 'Cornish Riviera Express' would have a correct 'Castle' class locomotive in green followed by its chocolate and cream coaches.

At Stirling Court, model trains caused one's first awareness of class distinctions. Not that we were permitted to have any of our trains there at school, every inch of the extremely limited floor space being already taken up with something or other, but in conversation we all provided details of the trains we had at home (I can still hear the convulsive sobs of a boy who, unwilling to spill the beans and then bullied into submission, had to confess that he had no trains) and this practice divided us neatly up into three classes. The upper class consisted of boys whose O gauge engines and carriages, and especially the former, all of which at that time worked by clockwork, came from a miraculous Holborn shop called Bassett-Lowke, incontestably superior to any other and with prices to prove it. Fortunately a kind godfather had given me a sturdy B-L tank engine, not as grand as an LNER express but still better than nothing and I made great play with its name and particulars.

The middle class consisted of boys who possessed Hornby trains, the rightly popular firm blossoming like anything in the 1920s and later, with an especially fine range of attractively coloured goods wagons and those long bogied ones (apt to be rather light and to topple over sideways at curves if the engine pulled too strongly). The lower class was, I regret to say, any train component that came from the now sadly defunct Gamages, though it was Gamages who scored finely in another field.

Towards the end of the Christmas term all the boys would write off to Gamages of Holborn for their giant (free) catalogue, which was packed with pictures of gifts of every sort, toys, games, camping equipment, chemistry sets, etc. During the 1920s Gamages must have despatched hundreds of thousands of their expensive catalogues to eager schoolboys. On occasions a boy would actually send off for something, accessories for trains, meccano parts, practical jokes, or an ant colony, but the catalogues were mainly used for window shopping, with now and again a choice of present to be acquired later from a kind aunt or uncle.

Collecting catalogues was in itself an important part of prep school life. 'I've got the new Harrods catalogue' or 'I've got the Rolls-Royce catalogue' were not idle boasts. Large firms seemed quite anxious to send expensive catalogues to 'Master . . .' at Belmont School, perhaps in the hope that they were appealing to tomorrow's buyers. There was a story, almost part of prep school folk-lore, of the company, said to be either Stratton Instone Ltd, or the coachmakers Thrupp and Maberley, who received a letter from a boy requesting a catalogue showing the latest models; he gave his name as 'Mr . . .' of '. . . House', without indicating, perhaps on purpose, that this was a school. As the address was near London, the head salesman decided to send, not the catalogue, but the latest luxury model itself. It was said that the small boy was in the middle of a French lesson when the school porter arrived to announce that 'Mr . . .'s Rolls-Royce Silver Ghost was at the front door!' After this episode writing off for catalogues was suspended for a period of time.

A popular pastime at Stirling Court was the racing of motor-cars. Photographs of Brooklands appeared constantly in the papers and we wanted a piece of the action. We fashioned a small block of wood into, roughly, the body of a racing-car, made cardboard wheels and fixed them to the chassis with pins (not easy), painted the ensemble in whatever pleasing colours we fancied and challenged each other. One end of one of the trestle tables at which we sat in our 'recreation room' (the tables could be ingeniously bolted together to form a stage for a play and its rehearsals, during which period we had to recreate ourselves in the classrooms) was raised, the support beneath it removed, and that end of the table lowered to the floor, thus providing a slippery sloping surface of a gradient, I suppose, of about one in four. Ideal. The cars careered down at high speed and then had to negotiate under their own momentum about six feet of floor. Wine-gum wagers enlivened the proceedings and needle finishes and alleged dead-heats produced terrific squabbles. And then suddenly we all got tired of motor-cars and went in for carefully constructed paper gliders (much grander things than paper darts) which, swooping about attractively overhead – soggy bread pellets would, if you were lucky, stick momentarily to the framework and then descend as a bomb – were launched from the highest available point in the room. This was the top of the upright piano and a sacred area in authority's eyes, the launcher standing upon it and to hell with the punishment if discovered – four of the best, or six if you had been caught before ('I will *not* have you repeatedly damaging my instrument' and a jolly phrase for mimics).

Elsewhere, other activities were in vogue, with here and there a surprising one.

> Crazes periodically sweep all schools; they start with an original idea, then slavish imitation. A boy arrived back at the beginning of one term with two knitting needles and a ball of wool. In no time this unmasculine innovation had aroused intense enthusiasm. Parents were bombarded with requests for knitting equipment, and soon the school resounded to the clack of knitting needles. Jagged multicoloured scarves besprinkled with dropped stitches began to make their appearance. Those who could not knit were regarded with disdain, while the boy who had mastered both plain and purl was admired by all. Then suddenly enthusiasm waned and everything returned to normal.

Different times of year brought different preoccupations.

There were the usual amusements according to the season. There was certainly a hammock-making season and a season for fighting with horse chestnuts and, in the summer, there were 'dabbing' cricket matches, in which one cheated, more or less outrageously, in favour of one's particular champion. There is a good deal to be done in this way without opening the eyes. One comes to know whereabouts on the board are the squares marked 'six' and those marked 'bowled' and the pencil can be wielded with considerable accuracy. I used to play this game with the future Bishop of Guildford and I do not believe that he was noticeably more honest than anyone else.

The teams for dab cricket were normally composed of the cream of the English and Australian players (at Stirling Court we were all tremendously keen on W. H. Ponsford) but in one school these recognized cricketers were alternated with All World Teams, for the selection of which history's and the bible's pages were freely drawn on.

TEAM

Attila the Hun (demon bowler)
The Venerable Bede (wicket-keeper)
Onan (backward point)
Julius Caesar (captain)
Pythagoras (square leg)
Hillard and Botting (opening batsmen)
Goliath (long leg)
Biggles (all-rounder)
Hercules (fast bowler)
Beethoven (left arm spinner)
  12th man: Ethelred the Unready
  Umpire: Pontius Pilate
  Scorer: Euclid

A rather curious keenness on stag-beetles has manifested itself down the years. Here we are in 1877:

> I find it hard to decide whether the rapture of making twenty at cricket against overhand bowling (not lobs from sisters) was greater or less than finding a stag-beetle on the palings, or in the early dawn of summer mornings going on tiptoe into the next dormitory and, after waking up my special friend, sitting on his bed, propped up with pillows and talking in whispers till there came the sound of the dressing-bell, which portended the entrance of the

matron. Then it was necessary to steal round the corner of his cubicle, and slide back into my own bed, there apparently to fall into a refreshing slumber, for to be caught out of bed before it was time to dress meant to be reported to Waterfield, who took a serious, and to me then, an unintelligible view of such an offence. But an hour's whispered conversation with a friend was worth that risk, indeed probably the risk added a certain savour to it. Or else it would be I who was awakened by the soft-stepping night-shirted figure, and moved aside in bed to give room for him to sit there, and there would be plans to be made, and then combining friendship with stag-beetles into one incomparable compound we would take the stag-beetles (for there were two of them, male and female called 'The Monarch of the Glen' and 'Queen') out of my washing basin, where they passed the night in optimistic attempts to climb its slippery sides, and refresh them with a basket of elm leaves and perhaps the half of a strawberry. They had to be put back into two match-boxes which were their travelling carriages before Jane the matron came round, for she had said that if ever she found stag-beetles in basins again she would throw them out of the window.

And again in more recent times.

The rearing of silkworms (eggs at sixpence a hundred from Gamages) to the detriment of the local mulberry trees, or stag-beetles with dignified surnames imprisoned in the dormitory wash-basins provided the nearest approach to nature study . . .

Artless diversions like 'high cockalorum' (spelling
optional) a sort of team leapfrog, shared the morning
break with rounders, 'he' and hopscotch ('hoppy').
The last named involved two 'sides', each with a
base; outside the bases, two combatants, hopping
on one leg with their arms folded, fought to shoulder
their opponents off their balance.

Also remembered are 'British Bulldog', 'chain he', 'French
and English', 'Twos and Threes' and 'Balcouriay', a kind
of 'ball he' with 'home' at each end of the asphalt playground
and 'he's' in the middle ready to throw a tennis ball to each
other in order to hit those running across. This was great
fun, especially when the headmaster or games master
joined in. Once you were hit you joined those in the middle.
The name presumably originated from the French 'balle'
and 'courir'.

In prep schools in general there was little of what might
be called serious smut and such merriment centred round
lavatories and defecation and the word 'bum'.

Prep school boys were, in my day, rather smutty
little brutes and we used to snigger and joke at
ridiculous little rhymes;

> Julius Caesar let off a breezer,
> His father tried to catch it.
> His mother stood behind the door
> And hit it with a hatchet.

> There was a bonnie Scotsman
> At the Battle of Waterloo
> The wind blew up his petticoats
> And showed his cockatoo;
> And when the war was over

> He went to beat the drum
> The wind blew up his petticoats
> And showed his dirty bum.

Schoolboy poets flourished and it is remarkable that a well-known end-of-term rhyme should have become popular, with many local variations, in almost every prep school in the land.

> Local customs prevailed, particularly towards the end of term, when cries of *Quis* (always pronounced 'Quiz') and *Ego* disposed of unwanted possessions . . . Naive jingles, such as 'Last week but one, take it all in fun' (thumping your hands), or 'Last week! don't squeak' (pinching your arms) were chanted along the passage. And the many local variants of the best known song;

> > This time next week, where shall I be?
> > Not in this acadamee;
> > No more Latin, no more Greek,
> > No more cane to make you squeak,
> > No more German, no more French,
> > No more standing on the bench,
> > No more greasy bread and butter,
> > No more water from the gutter,
> > No more spiders in my tea
> > Making googly eyes at me!

And there were 'More-days' in a Sussex prep school. A competition with a prize for the most original drawing depicting something that was to happen in so many days (or hours, or minutes) to coincide with the approach of the end of term. The number would be altered on the drawing daily as the great day approached.

A great deal of reading went on and at Stirling Court the competition for the latest *Sapper* ('Bags I!') was intense. When we had completed our 'prep' for the evening, we were permitted to read our own books and a very agreeable and rewarding time it was.

> We all read boys' magazines and comics. At Belmont (1922–26) I read *B.O.P.*, *Chums*, old bound copies of *Punch* and all sorts of novels; Stevenson, Henty, P. G. Wodehouse school stories, Captain Charles Gilson, Marryat and others. Also Lewis Carroll and whatever else I could find in the meagre School Library, like the *Railway Children*.

One school had some beautifully bound copies of the *Illustrated London News*. They dated back to the early years of the century and the most popular were those dealing with the First World War.

6 p.m.

Every four weeks or so, 'prep' was abandoned in favour of a lecture or demonstration (if it was a chemical one, there was always the happy chance of an explosion) or a performance of some sort – hand-bell ringing perhaps, and those delightfully tinkley tunes. How the hearts of headmasters and their wives, resident in remote country areas and before the days of easy transport, must have sunk at the realization that the lecture would not end until seven p.m. ('Any more questions?') at the earliest and that the lecturer would then have to be given dinner ('Another rissole?') and then be accommodated for the night, with breakfast ('More haddock?') to follow.

The lectures were invariably illustrated with lantern slides projected onto a screen by what was then called a 'magic lantern', an unco-operative instrument with a will of its own. A junior master, perched upon a dais, inserted the slides as signalled by the lecturer, either with one of those clicker things or by thumping on the floor with the pointer with which he was urging his audience to admire Botticelli's brushwork or the temples at Paestum. Schoolboys waited in breathless anticipation for one of the slides to stick or for Chartres Cathedral to come juddering on upside down (ironical applause was rash, the applauders being, need one say, beaten 'after prayers').

Saturday evening entertainments became more ambitious. There were frequent lectures by visitors who were distinguished or interesting or both. Once, the school was treated to a demonstration of ju-jitsu; Dr Barnardo, whose son was at the school, often lectured on his homes; and on one occasion the Revd W. C. Procter spoke on the manufacture of soap in Widnes. There were, too, impersonations and recitations, juggling and conjuring ('Mr Warren's entertainment was refreshingly humorous throughout, and entirely free from vulgarity'), ventriloquism and marionettes. A celebrity played the piano blindfold, with the instrument covered by a cloth. There were demonstrations of the phonograph and the kinematograph. Mr Charles King and company performed a playlet which 'possessed no special merit'.

As a lecture high spot, the manufacture of soap in Widnes would be hard to equal.

Then there were the travelling lecturers and performers who were often retired servicemen. They showed us slides of their travels in Asia Minor and we hooted with mirth when the slides got mixed up or the lantern bulb exploded. Some brought animals with them, hawks, Saint Bernards and things in little cages. The *pièce de résistance* was a magician who arrived in a trunk. The prefects carried the trunk onto the stage amid great applause; when the trunk had been unstrapped, there emerged a little old man who performed some quite ordinary tricks with silk handkerchiefs and playing cards.

But he left the way he came, by trunk, and that for us was sheer magic. I think he called himself Count Lemski, but he was probably a retired shopkeeper from Bedminster.

The winter term often ended with the school play – two performances, the first (really a glorified dress rehearsal) being for the members of the domestic staff and assorted local friends, the second being for the school and any parents who could come (silver collection for Dr Barnardo's Homes).

The standard of play production and acting in some schools is now quite incredibly high but time was when there were a number of entertaining imperfections to look out for. The excited faces peering through the central gap in the dark green curtains. The loud whisperings and last minute instructions and the preliminary twitching of the curtain cords before the vigorous and deafening rattling back of the brass curtain-rings. The dramatic exits which get held up by doors being pushed when they should have been pulled. That moment when the prompter, carried away by the action, crosses his or her legs and a large shoe becomes visible jutting from the wings. The beetroot make-ups. The wrist-watches retained by mistake in Shakespearean scenes and looking especially bizarre on Lady Macbeth when sleep-walking or the dying Hamlet. The performer, anxiously awaiting his cue, who is seen to be silently mouthing the words of his cue-giver. The inability just to stand quite still when not actively engaged in plot or dialogue, and the distracting rocking to and fro from foot to foot. The sidelong glances at the audience. Above all, the inability to *listen*, often just as telling as speaking.

A headmaster has kindly left us his notes after a successful production, comparing it favourably, though not in all respects, with some earlier efforts.

> The murderers' daggers and suicides' swords came through the victims' bodies clean and bright, not red with gore as we used to contrive them . . . Then of course we no longer have the mishaps and incongruities and curious incidents and asides which roused the audience to enthusiastic shouts in the old days; the wig coming off at a critical moment, the manifest liveliness of dead warriors, the shouts from the wings – 'Pull him off!', 'Get into the limelight, you idiot!' Everything goes smoothly now, as doubtless it should. The curtain no longer falls on an actor's head; no stray figures rush on to pick up hat or wig or sword; wooden swords are no longer broken on helm or shield; no one emerges from a battle with a genuine black eye.

In some quarters it is now fashionable, if that be the word, to sneer at Gilbert and Sullivan, but who can dispute the fact that for a prep school production there is nothing better? For one thing, the entire school gets involved one way or another. The boys are speaking admirable dialogue and learning words they never knew before. They find themselves getting unlaboured laughs. The female roles present no sort of difficulty. The costumes and sets, home-made, encourage ingenuity. And there is the music! This lends itself splendidly to being arranged for two pianos. Who could ask more? And for the audience there is an enjoyment not always available from amateur performances.

> The applause that usually greeted the first appear-ance of the 'girls' chorus was a well deserved tribute to the work of the army of dressers behind the

scenes; but on their first exit the chorus would report delightedly and excitedly, 'We got clapped!' In the dressers' department it was as well to be ready for anything – from the two fairies just inspected and next moment locked in mortal combat on the floor, to the lovesick maiden who decided to while away the interval by using 'her' wig as a skipping rope.

A daring innovation at the Dragon School supplies a pleasing moment.

A year later a somewhat controversial venture, *The Beggar's Opera*, took the place of the more normal Gilbert and Sullivan. Some sought to query the choice of play on moral grounds, but at least the junior boy who remarked to his mother on the way out, 'What a lot of secretaries Captain Macheath had,' did not seem to have suffered untold damage.

Bedtime

Bedtimes vary from school to school, and are scaled according to the age of the boy, but it is safe to say that from about 7 p.m. onwards somebody somewhere is on his way upstairs, often to a dormitory called, in grateful remembrance of helpful nautical moments, either 'Frobisher' or 'Drake' or 'Jellicoe' or 'Beatty' (are they ever perhaps changed or, like Stalin, demoted?). Matrons, and especially under-matrons, are busy in the bathrooms, encouraging washing. The master on duty is parading the dormitories, for this is another period of the day when bullies can be active, and a boy who is unhappy, for whatever reason, is most likely to display his distress at this hour. Prior to mounting the stairs, some boys have had one of the best of all juvenile treats.

The boys' room has changed only in the density of its population. In its early years it made a wonderful setting for the headmaster's story telling on Saturday nights, with the lights out and the firelight flickering on the circle of rapt faces. Some of the stories were original; others came from various authors, such as M. R. James. All were related as personal experiences, and they sometimes ended with the production from his pocket of some small object that had been worked into the story, and was now offered and readily accepted as convincing proof of its truth – even a stone picked up from the drive outside.

In the masters' common room, usually a fairly bleak sanctum with a fusty musty smell of its own, some of the staff are probably getting on with their end-of-term reports. I doubt if there are anywhere ruder school reports than those supplied by Eton beaks ('Idle and means to be. Sits a lumpish figure in school' is a fair example) and some prep schools permit sharper remarks than others.

Geography.	He does well to find his way home.
Writing.	Now that his writing has improved, we have been able to discover how very little he knows.
Writing.	The dawn of legibility in your son's handwriting reveals his total inability to spell.
Swimming.	Tends to sink.
Scripture.	Foggy.
Arithmetic.	The ice is broken. That is all that can be said.
General.	It is not any abnormal weight of mind that prevents the upward growth of his body.
Singing.	Flat, but very plucky.

An interesting report was once given about a boy who had previously been taught the piano by a succession of ladies.

Music.	He has had five mistresses in four years and picked up a lot of bad habits.

Two reports, under the 'General Conduct' heading, have survived from the distant past. One is by an assistant master.

> I hope to break Alfred of the habit of saying 'What?' whenever spoken to, also of the peculiarity of never doing anything that he is told – nor of taking the least notice of any word of command until it has been repeated several times.

And this one from a headmaster shows a really splendid disregard for the conventions.

> His frankness over his boys' intellectual ability was matched by a frankness over other matters; 'The obstacle he has to overcome is the lack of any present or prospective discomfort in life, such as could be staved off by some exertions of his own. In fact he suffers from a malady for which it is difficult to provide a remedy; he is a rich man's only son. The effects of this malady may be shaken off when Clifford develops a stronger sense of duty as regards the talents committed to his charge . . . If you want him to study with all his heart, with all his soul and with all his strength, you should go bankrupt!'

Sometimes the report-writers cease their labours, light a pipe (the percentage of pipe-smokers among prep school staffs, all contentedly and soothingly puffing away, is often very high, a fact that is in no way remarkable) and swap the day's howlers.

What did a consul wear? A pagoda.
What is meant by an ultimatum? A sort of disinfectant.
What is a sorcerer? A man who makes china.

Who was Rider Haggard? A famous jockey.
Name one of Milton's poems. Gray's Elegy.

Or perhaps there is an exchange of what one might call
slightly schoolmasterly jokes.

At one staff meeting someone raised the question
of boys who ask to 'be excused' in class. 'Any
schoolmaster who knows his job,' said the head,
'can tell whether such a request is genuine.' 'Well
headmaster,' replied one member of staff, 'personally I was engaged here as a teacher, not a water
diviner.'

From time to time a headmaster will jot down items of news
that are considered to be suitable material for the school
magazine. All too seldom does a paragraph like the following fall into his lap. The item refers to the visit, unexpected,
of the King and Queen, resulting in an annual 'Whole
Holiday' on every 18th June from 1942 until the school
closed down.

Twice during the Second World War the royal
train 'stabled' at Featherstone Park station; and
one Sunday evening after dinner the King and
Queen decided to call on Featherstone Castle and
were confronted at the door by the headmaster, my
predecessor, with a long carving-knife in his hand
(he had been cutting the staff's ham in the hall
within!). The King and Queen, delighted by their
odd reception, asked if they might meet all the
boys. The latter were in the process of going to bed
and a priceless 'pyjama parade' took place on the
tennis court beside the dormitory wing. When they
had shaken hands with everyone the royal couple
asked if there were any more boys; 'Yes,' came the

reply, 'There are two patrols having a scout camp on the hillside'; so the King and Queen climbed up to the group of tents and surprised two grubby sets of boys cooking sausages over their camp-fires.

Which wartime headmaster cannot recall vastly irritating and purposeless questions from official quarters?

Although such things as food rationing were, in 1940, infinitely more efficient than in 1914–18, bureaucracy still, inevitably, enjoyed a field day. I still recall two questions I was asked. One was 'how many hours of work do you do a week?' to which I replied, '168.' Entirely accurate, because responsibility cannot be measured by the clock. The other, 'How many hot drinks were served in your school during the year ending . . ?' was a poser. Luckily, the charming young lady at the ministry, whom I asked whether to count in a hot cup of tea grown cold while I answered the telephone, agreed to my entering the school telephone number, multiplying by three and adding two noughts. One day, perhaps, these valuable statistics will be excavated from some dusty subterranean stratum of a ministry file.

Not all visitors to school are royal ones, but doubtless in the following case the Dragon School was quite happy to put up with second best.

On the day of the fête the weather was fine, or nearly so; and John Betjeman, as official opener, arrived by helicopter and at once expressed his keen pleasure at having just landed on the cricket square and so prevented any cricket being played for one afternoon.

It was very far from being Sir John's first experience of the school. Before the staff graduated from motor bikes to cars the headmaster and his wife could be seen out riding together, as is shown in this effort by a twelve-year-old future Poet Laureate:

Hum and May went out one day
On a motor-bike painted vermilion,
Hum was the knut of the latest cut.
And May was the girl on the pillion.

Day's End

Lights go out in the dormitories ('No more talking! Williamson, *will* you shut up!') matron heaves her last heavy sigh of the day (Medlicott's 'temp' has shot up to 102.4), the staff are sitting down to an unidentifiable brown mound that can only be stew, the cook reports to the headmaster's wife that she is 'worried' about one of the maids (Parker, clearly heavily *enceinte*), a mother has rung up to ask if Gerald can 'drop' algebra ('He *does* seem to hate it so!'), the headmaster has decided that he must at last put the fees up, and eventually silence falls, all activity ceases, and the school sleeps.

Parents, those heavily-burdened and courageous persons, are always optimistic about sending their boys to prep schools and, no matter what their own harsh experiences may have been, take the rosiest of views about such schools at the present time.

Parents forever console themselves when they part with their boys with the thought that schools are so much better now than they were; there is no bullying, the food is good, ample and wholesome; hygiene is properly understood; the linen is aired; the clothes are sensible, if expensive; the masters are reasonable, intelligent and up-to-date: they have not forgotten they were once boys themselves; they are men of the world; they know that there are more things in heaven and earth than cricket and football. It may be so; but the truth about any individual boy is not known, after the first few days of his school experience when he will sometimes write and ask to be taken away, until he is grown up; for boys never tell their parents the truth about their school life. They couldn't if they would, for they are without any standard of comparison and any apparatus of criticism, and they take for granted certain things which might make their parents swoon with horror, whereas certain things which the parents might well approve of they regard with disgust.

Those were the views of Maurice Baring over sixty years ago and who could say that things have in any way changed?

On one thing all must agree – the extraordinary sharpness of adult memories concerning the years when they were growing up, from, say, seven to seventeen. As regards one's own prep school days, all is vividly there and becomes, in some strange way, clearer with every year that passes – the fun, the staff, the rows, the tears, the classes, the larks, the troubles, the few successes and the many failures, and most of all the almost constant anxieties of one sort or another. I can truthfully say that of all the frights in my life, and there have been many, none has ever equalled the moment in 1920 when I lost my front collar stud, with the breakfast gong thirty seconds away.

One little knew then how clearly one was going to recall it all, but one exceptional small boy knew otherwise.

There was one evening in the hall of late golden light and the unmistakable noise of the marbles ringing and rolling on the wood floor, hundreds of them, and the voices of my school mates, all in a state of pleasure and purposeful activity, and I was running round, not even, I think, playing 'he', just swinging up on to the platform off the parallel bars. I looked down the hall and I thought in a flash, I will remember this all my life. It came to me as certainly as one running foot before the other touched ground, and then I was off again. But it was true.